Bringing Heaven Home

We Were Never Meant to Do It Alone

By Brent C. Satterfield, Ph.D.

CONTENTS

ACKNOWLEDGMENTS

To Jenn and my children for walking with me as these experiences reconstructed my world. To Jeff Lark for the countless hours spent reviewing the manuscript and extracting details from my memory. To Natalia Yates, Dana Parker, and Hannah Foust for reviewing every word and giving me the focus to finish the task. To the many others who helped shape the events behind this book. To the readers and those who are awakening who do the real work in shifting the patterns in this world.

I experienced heaven - multiple times. Each time was unique, with Jesus showing me more than my cultural container of Christianity could hold. It's hard to think that it could ever be difficult to talk about the love that exists in God's presence, but it is. Even the people you think would be most interested often don't want to hear it. As much as we say we do, we value predictability more, and the moment that God's love contradicts our long-held beliefs or traditions, we want nothing to do with it. The unknown can be scary, and the more we experience God's love, the more it pushes us into the unpredictability of the unknown. But what if God's love is bigger than our traditions? What if heaven is bigger than the visions of just one person or culture?

Bringing Heaven Home is my journey of discovering how much bigger heaven actually is than the cultural understandings I grew up with. This happens through a series of experiences I had with God and heaven over a period of years, including five crossovers similar to near-death experiences. Each experience peeled back a new layer of understanding and perception of God, as God took me from a religious perspective of fear, guilt, and shame into the embrace of His absolute love and acceptance. They also led me to experience the contribution of multiple cultures around our collective understanding of God. Taken individually, they are beautiful snapshots of heaven. Altogether, they form a panorama of the journey of human awareness in its awakening to the moment-to-moment experience of God's love.

One of the most intense aspects of awakening is the terrible feeling of complete aloneness that often occurs as we realize truths about ourselves and God that challenge the best understandings of past generations. It is my hope in sharing these words that you know that you are never alone – that wherever you are, you can feel a warm hug all around you – and I hope that this book does just that. It is my hope that we can find courage in each other's vulnerability, enough to take the next step on our journey. I also hope that we can deepen humanity's conversations on unity and what it will take not just for an individual to wake up, but for the whole world.

I organized this book into five sections, one for each cross-over experience. There is a chapter in each section that is named for the experience (e.g. First Experience, etc). I did this so that if you are like me, you can jump straight to the experiences and leave the backstory for later. Although, you may find that the real message is in the journey more than the experiences themselves.

A Prayer and a Plane Ride

"Father," I prayed. "I finished writing the book, but I'm afraid of showing my heart. I'm afraid of the hurt and suffering in this world. I don't want to be hurt again."

In the background, I could hear the airline attendants calling out instructions for boarding our flight. I continued my silent prayer as I grabbed my bag and headed toward the gate, "I still struggle with my life – is this even a message that should be told? I mean, how can the imperfection of my words communicate the beauty in what I've seen? I don't even know how to interpret all I've seen. I could use some help to know what to do, and it needs to be obvious enough to get through my head." As I finished the prayer, I knew I didn't have to think about the book anymore. My trust was simple. If there was anything more I should do, it would show up without me having to look for it.

As I boarded the plane and made my way toward my seat, I noticed a young man in the seat beside mine. He looked to be in his early thirties with a definite eye for fashion. He was hard at work, pouring over a manuscript that completely filled a three-inch, three-ring binder. The manuscript revealed heavy edits he and others had already made in a computer program, but it seemed he was now going the extra mile making comments between the lines by hand.

On long plane rides, I never know the temperament of the person I will be sitting next to. Most won't meet your eyes, but a few are looking for conversation to pass the time. I figured I'd roll the dice with a little friendly teasing.

"Looks like fun," I remarked somewhat dryly, referring to his work.

As an inventor and a DNA scientist, I had worked on editing plenty of technical documents in the past. While I had no idea what he was working on, any document that size with that many edits had to be what I teasingly referred to as "fun."

He looked up as if to make sure I was actually addressing him. "Actually, yes," he responded with unexpected enthusiasm.

I was caught off guard with his response; I couldn't think of a reply. But as it turned out, I didn't need to.

"These are the final edits before I get my book published," he elaborated.

"Oh, so you're a writer?" I asked.

"No, I'm actually a film producer for movies up to a forty-million-dollar budget."

"And you're writing a book?" I prompted, a little confused.

"Yeah, this is my first book; it's a Christian inspirational about my granddad. My agent found a publisher willing to pay in advance for the concept and then I hired a best-selling novelist to do the bulk of the writing. Now I'm making final comments and revisions."

"I've done a lot of family history," I said, "but I can't even get my family to read it. How are you getting paid to publish a book about your granddad, especially when you've never written one before?"

He looked thoughtful for a moment and said, "As a film producer, I like to think I have an eye for a story. And my granddad's story is as good as they come. He left a career as a famous musician to be a high-school teacher in a small town. The story is in the struggles he went through in making that decision, and the way that he ended up changing his community as a result of his choice."

He paused for a moment to show me a little of the structure in the book. "See how I'm using dialogue? It makes the story and the plotline develop like fiction, but all the dialogue comes out of the journals he kept, so it's still true-to-life."

"Oh," I said. "So, this should grab the reader like a fiction novel, only it has that extra depth that comes from also being true."

"Exactly," he replied. "The inspirational book market is constantly looking for true stories that the everyday person can relate to."

After making this remark, he turned the conversation back to me, "So, what do you do?"

I paused. Most people don't have to hesitate in answering this question, but the truth was, I wasn't entirely sure at the moment. And I realized that maybe this chance meeting was not so chance after all. It was possible it was the answer to the prayer I had uttered just before boarding the plane.

"Four years ago, I stepped down as the CEO of a biotech company." Searching for the right words I continued, "I did it to follow a, well, sort of a spiritual impression to study faith healing with people from different cultures."

"That sounds interesting," he responded. "Is that what you do now?"

"Umm, not really. I wrote a book on what I learned, but I published that over a year ago. Now I'm working on another book idea. I'm just not sure what to do with it yet."

"Oh, really?" he asked. "What's this new book about?"

"Well, during the time I was travelling, I had a few experiences of heaven, kind of like near-death experiences."

He did a double take, "Wait, you saw heaven? You mean like, you saw Jesus?"

"Yeah," I answered. "And a whole lot more. Unlike most accounts I've heard of people who've seen the other side, I had multiple experiences."

He looked at me a moment as if trying to gauge if I was serious, and then he stated, "That's incredible. I've never met anyone who's seen the other side even once, let alone several times! So, what'd you see?"

I started to tell him that it was a long story, but then I recalled we were stuck together on a plane for the next several hours. Besides, just after telling God He was going to have to intervene for me to publish my book, I sat down next to this young man who was in the process of publishing a Christian inspirational and was also a movie producer. Was this part of the answer I was looking for?

However, even if this moment was divinely orchestrated, I still had several reasons for hesitating. As my dad taught me when I was little, there are three subjects you never talk about in polite society: money, politics, and religion. Out of those three, the most sensitive is religion. Even Jesus emphasized this idea when he taught that we shouldn't cast our pearls before swine.[1] Like a young person sharing their love for the first time, it is sweeter when it is received by someone who values it. The more tender and sacred something is to us, the more vulnerable we are to harm from sharing that part of us with someone who does not appreciate it. Spiritual experiences, not surprisingly, tend to be the most tender of all.

For this reason, those who come back from near-death experiences and related visions of heaven often have trouble reintegrating into the world. They have seen that which has never entered into the hearts of humankind and have been exposed to a love in which there is no comparison in this world. It has changed their entire being and the way they see everything. Back on earth, people still see through the same filter. They are not so kind; they are not so loving. It hurts to realize how few people there are willing to truly hear the beauty of experiences on the other side.

Even Todd Burpo, the pastor who recounted his son's experience with Jesus in *Heaven is for Real*, reported difficulties in telling the story. Not everyone from his religious community was welcoming to even the idea of it. And he was the pastor of people who supposedly *shared* his beliefs!

I didn't know much about the religious beliefs or background of the man sitting beside me, and I didn't know how he might receive what I had experienced. But I did know the odds of us meeting in this way at this time were too low to be chance alone.

_____

[1] Matthew 7:6

I also knew he seemed genuinely interested. So, I resolved to do what I often do when talking with others, tell a little of the story and see if they ask for more. There wasn't much harm in that.

"My first experience helped me to see that heaven is very different than how we see things on earth," I told him.

"What do you mean by that?" he asked.

"Well, specifically there was no judgment," I recalled. I went deeper into the memory as the feeling began to surface within me again. He waited patiently for me to continue.

"I was loved in a way that I've never known in this life," I said as I sought for better vocabulary to convey the feeling and yet simultaneously only share the smallest of details. "I saw the perfection in even the parts of my life I thought could never be healed. In fact, those moments were the most perfect of all."

There was silence. You could hear the soft blowing of the air-conditioning unit overhead.

"No judgment?" he asked tentatively. He looked away as though reflecting on something that had troubled him in the past. "I'm a Christian and I believe God is a lot more merciful than most people think He is, but are you saying God doesn't judge at all?"

"Not in my experience," I said.

I watched him to see how he would respond. I was well aware of what most churches taught and it was a lot different from what I was telling him now. He nodded for me to continue, so I did. "For me, He was only love. And I'm not alone in that thought."

"What do you mean by that?" he asked.

"Well," I continued, "after my experiences I went back and read hundreds of near-death experiences that others have had. I also met quite a few people who were willing to share their experiences of the other side with me. I wanted to know how much of what I saw has been seen by others."

I paused and looked him in the eye. I wanted to make sure he understood the next point. "The number one thing they all say, regardless of the religion they come from, is that they were surprised by the complete lack of judgment they experienced."

The stewardess passed by dropping off water. He used the opportunity to gather his thoughts, then said, "I live in California now and work in the movie industry. Almost everyone there is from other religions. What about them?"

I thought I knew what he was getting at. Many conservative religions believe that theirs is the only path approved by God. People like my new friend who have positive experiences with God are conflicted by the contradiction they feel between God's love and the rigidity exhibited by some religions. I imagined he was asking me if I had seen anything that would shed light on that subject.

"Umm..." I hesitated. "My experiences suggest that heaven is bigger than what most people think."

I paused, looking for any hint in his eyes what his background would allow him to believe. I've learned that oftentimes in such moments, the words I need seem to come out of nowhere. Right then, two popular Biblical passages jumped into my mind that I thought he might have heard during Sunday services, and I referenced them to expound on my previous thought, "You see, Jesus didn't come to condemn the world but to save it from its own judgment.[2] He even said that in his 'Father's house are many mansions.'[3] I think we'll be surprised by how big heaven is when we get there."

He stared straight ahead while turning his pencil over in his hands. He seemed to be reflecting on what this might mean for the spiritual paradigms he grew up with. At length he said, "That makes sense to me. I mean, I don't always understand the way others practice their religions, but they seem to believe as much as I do."

---

[2] "For God sent not his Son into the world to condemn the world; but that the world through him might be saved." John 3:17

[3] John 14:2

I nodded encouragingly for him to keep putting his thoughts into words. He added, "I just can't understand how God could throw them into Hell when they're putting all their faith and hope in Him, even if they call Him by another name."

I shrugged and smiled in agreement as he sat back seemingly resolved on the matter. Then he looked up at me again, changing the subject. "So, did you actually die five times?"

I chuckled at his directness before replying, "No. I'm not sure if I actually died any of the times. I mean, I wasn't taken to a hospital intensive care unit for any of them."

He looked at me curiously as if waiting for further explanation. So I continued, "But in my second experience, I really thought I was going to die."

I opened the airline's generic bag of pretzels and thought back to that moment. He motioned for me to continue and I said, "There was this beautiful energy that filled my being."

I stopped again to reflect deeper on the experience. It was not a feeling that I had ever felt before. But every time I thought back to it, the memory seemed to rush back in a way that allowed me to feel it all over again. "I felt… I felt completely embraced by God's love. You know, it was kind of like the tingling of pins and needles when your leg falls asleep, but throughout my entire body… and thousands of times more intense."

I looked in his eyes. He was watching me intently, so I went on, "I thoroughly enjoyed it until it moved into my heart."

I thought about the surprise I had when I could no longer feel my lips and when my whole body had gone numb except for the intense exploding feeling in my heart. I ate another pretzel before adding, "It felt like my heart was moving in a million directions all at once with severely arrhythmic beating, and I thought *This isn't fun anymore – I'm having a heart attack – I'm going to die!*"

My fellow passenger lost no time with a follow-up question, "Is that the experience when you saw Jesus – the one where there was no judgment?"

"No," I said and then hesitated. I had encountered Jesus in several experiences, this one in particular lasting several hours, but where to begin? "There was no judgment in any of my experiences. But... I guess it was in my first experience that it impacted me most profoundly. This one, where I thought I was going to die, was my second experience."

I looked at him to see if he had anything else to ask, but he gestured for me to continue. He seemed to be enjoying the conversation. So, I added, "But I did see Jesus in my second experience too. It was by far my longest experience as I was on the other side for several hours."

I took a sip of water and then went back to his previous question about dying, "I know I didn't die in my first experience."

He pushed his hair back as I continued, "At the time, I was with a woman who had four near-death experiences, the first in an airplane crash."

His eyebrows went up at that and I smiled inwardly. Not only is surviving an airplane crash incredible, but talking about dying in an airplane crash while being on an airplane seemed a little ironic.

I explained, "One of the gifts she came back with was the ability to help someone cross over without having to die to get there. That was the first time I felt that pins and needles loss of bodily sensation, but just without the life-threatening intensity the way it happened the second time."

He seemed dumbfounded, "Umm... So, a woman had four near-death experiences – and she helped you have your own experience?"

Once started, his questions tumbled out faster than I could respond, "What happened there? Can you tell me about it? How did you meet her, and what led up to it?"

The man was practically glowing with enthusiasm and had completely forgotten his manuscript. I knew this was going to be a long conversation. But it was also going to be enjoyable to talk with someone who really wanted to know. As much as there are few things more painful than sharing your pearls with someone who isn't prepared to receive them, there are also few things more joyous than relating those details to someone who is excited about them. I smiled as I began to recollect the details leading up to that first experience.

Part 1

God is Love

Chapter 1

Born Again

I was depressed and frequently suicidal. But maybe seeing God doesn't come from having a perfect home, or a perfect grasp on life. Maybe, it happens despite these things – so that we can learn what it truly means to be loved. Ironically, in the painful years that followed my experiences where I pined to have the heavens open again, I have pondered that the opposite might also be true. Maybe not finding God when we most long for deliverance is so we can learn just how profoundly we are connected.

Each of us has a slightly different idea of what it means to be loved. For my child-self, the feeling of love was in the sharp sting of dad's belt whenever I crossed a boundary and in the way he completely overlooked the 100% score on a test asking, "Why did you miss the extra-credit?" It was in the emotional obligation to be aware of what mom was feeling and make sure she was always happy. Despite loving parents, or perhaps because of them, is it any wonder that later in life I looked for the love of God in the same way? That I believed that His love was found in strict religious boundaries and the need to always do more to make Him happy? As is the case for so many of us, I was not aware of what I had not experienced, of that for which there is no earthly description. I only knew love as I had experienced it.

As a teenager, I pushed back against what I saw as an impossible standard. I ran away for a brief time and became involved with people and circumstances that broke my parents' heart. Although my parents never knew it, I tried to commit suicide several times during this period. When I turned eighteen, I felt God's presence for the first time after a night of sobbing from a drug-induced experience turned bad.

This surprised me because I had been decidedly atheistic prior to this experience. I was not raised religious and I had no previous inclinations. But there was no question in my mind as to the contrast I experienced between a hellacious nightmare and the overwhelming peace that enveloped me as I felt a loving Intelligence outside my own. It was an enveloping peace so tangible and so completely outside of any possible experience I could conceive that it utterly changed my life. Even though this was not the level of the crossover experiences I would have later in life, it was an intimation of the many tender embraces to come that profoundly shaped my life. Suddenly, I had a purpose – I was not alone; there was some Divine Presence and I needed to know who or what It was. This became my purpose.

I lost all interest in everything that rebellious teenage boys crave and sought out spiritual truth. Although I was not raised religious, I grew up in a southern community where cornbread and Jesus were often used in the same sentence. So, the only God I knew was a Christian God, and it was to Him I turned at that time.

I started by going to every Christian denomination in my neighborhood. However, when I spoke to the pastors, they did not seem to understand the experience I had. Perhaps I simply was unlucky in the churches I chose to visit. However, my young mind wanted to know how I could find God in churches where the pastors had no real experience with Him. My ongoing efforts to be "good" weren't bringing me any answers either. So, what could I do to find them?

I resolved on a stratagem that had as much intelligence as is characteristic of an eighteen-year-old boy. I reasoned, *If God talked to me when I was dabbling in what is "wrong," then maybe I should like, really do what is wrong to find Him again.* In something that has been both a strength and a weakness for me throughout my life, I was willing to do whatever it took and to pay any price to find meaning in my existence. The translucent boundaries in this aquarium called life almost compelled me to search them out and see what they were made of.

As silly as it may sound, there was some sincere logic to my approach. The only time God had ever shown an interest in me or made Himself known to me was when I was misbehaving. So, as child psychologists will tell you, if the only way a child can get your attention is through misbehavior, then they will do it.[4] What children truly crave, and my newfound relationship with God was no exception, is love through attention. What I couldn't get from my dad, I determined to get from God, and I was determined to get His attention through any means necessary!

That ended about as well as you might imagine. The summer I graduated from high school, some friends and I broke into a home to collect "souvenirs," the term we used for the stolen tokens of our presumed bravery. I took a revolutionary-war era muzzle loader. In a twist of fate, it turned out the muzzle-loader belonged to the judge's secretary. Much to my surprise it was also worth over $10,000, leading to a charge of grand-theft firearm which carried a minimum sentence of three years in prison. A small white boy like me wouldn't survive two minutes in a southern prison, let alone three years, so I accepted a plea deal to lower the charge to burglary of a dwelling while armed. That translated to a sentence of just under a year that could be served in the relative safety of the local county jail. During that year I spent staring at the white walls of my cell, I had plenty of time to reflect on God's nature. I spent my days meditating and reading every religious text I could get my hands on.

After getting out of jail, I was still unable to find the answers my heart was craving to make real change. So, my life took another dive into even worse situations. By the time I was twenty-one, things had gotten so bad that God opened a vision to me showing me that if I did not change, I would either end up dead or in prison for the rest of my life. I say vision, but vision is only the closest word for what it was. It was an understanding that was communicated to me more clearly than any visual image. It was like seeing eternity compounded upon itself in the understanding of a single moment. It was a perception so profound that it was accompanied by visual images that supported the understanding. But it was not the fear of prison or of death that truly took hold of my heart. It was a vision of what

[4] See *Power of Positive Parenting: A Wonderful Way to Raise Children* by Dr. Glenn Latham.

my experience would be like after this life. I saw the same suffering that then gripped my heart expand into eternity, becoming heavier and more unbearable with the compounding of each passing moment. It was crushing; it was overwhelming. I knew it was time to change. And what was more, I knew that God knew that I knew. There was no denying this moment.

I was convinced the hellish feelings I was experiencing were a result of denying my Christian heritage, and I wanted to know how I could reconcile my life with Jesus. I also knew that I had offered my life to Him several times in the past and not kept my promise. The first time I was in sixth grade. I told Him I would give Him the rest of my life if He would heal my grandad who had an incurable cancer the size of a football in his stomach. I had already lost one grandpa the year before; I wasn't ready to lose another. However, when my grandad was unexpectedly admitted to a clinical trial a week later and completely cured of his cancer, I promptly forgot my promise. Even in my prayers to find Him before I went to jail, I could now see the lack of real intent to honor my promise. The changes I made lasted for just a short time. I saw that was why I had not received an answer then. I was too addicted to my life to have any real intention of change. I wanted answers that justified my desires, not to truly know God. I now knew that if I was going to receive an answer, I had to pray differently than I had ever prayed before. These had to be more than just words from my lips. I had to pray from a space within my heart that came from true commitment to make any change that God asked. Even with all this awareness, I still took more than an hour to ponder it over before making a decision. I knew once the decision was made, I could not go back on it. I had to think through the full cost before making the commitment. It was with these thoughts that I finally offered the first prayer from my lips with real intent.

"What do I need to do?" I asked God imploringly. On the face of the vision He had just shown me and the intention in my heart, I had no question He would answer.

Unlike the times when I had prayed before, this time I heard a voice clearly saying, "You need to be baptized." With that response, I felt hope suddenly rekindle in my soul. It was like the light of a small flame kindled within the pitch-black interior of the darkest cave. My mistakes were not too much – I was being given another chance! I saw this baptism as a fresh start into a new understanding and way of life.

"But where should I be baptized?" I asked. My confusion was real. I elaborated, as if God needed me to explain what I meant, "If you are real enough to talk to me then you are real enough to care where I go to church. Out of all the churches out there, where should I be baptized?"

After I spent some time pleading, the voice responded with a question of its own, "What church is the true church?"

"I don't know," I said with a hint of frustration. I was having a conversation that few people can imagine and yet God seemed to be failing to understand what I needed. "That's why I'm asking!"

"Then, which brings salvation," the voice asked calmly. "Jesus or the church?"

"Jesus," I said promptly.

Immediately, the voice repeated the first question, "Then, which church is the true church?"

In that moment, multiple understandings came into my heart all at once even as I said the words, "The church of Jesus Christ." First, I knew that the true church was that group of people who sincerely followed the light with all their hearts, regardless of the religion they belonged to. Second, I knew where God wanted me to be baptized because of the faith of those I would associate with.

Even after receiving this answer, I was still terrified. My life felt like one big mistake. I had denied God and ended up miserable. There were literally people who wanted to kill me. I felt God had judged me and found me wanting. As I learned later, this did not mean that God actually was judging me. However, in the state of mind I was in at the time, it was the only way I could make sense of what was happening. Real or not, I sincerely believed He was giving me one last chance to shape up; I did not feel there was any hope for me if I ever made another mistake. The intensity of this belief was probably a large part of what gave me the power to change my life so dramatically. I needed a super-rigid cocoon of understanding for the kind of butterfly I was to become.

I asked with some fear, "God, I know we're not supposed to ask for a sign. But, how do I know this is really you? I can't afford to make another mistake."

In that precise moment, there was a flash of brilliant light throughout my whole being. It filled me with a feeling of holiness so intense that all of my questioning and doubt instantly departed. I knew exactly what I needed to do and for the first time in my life, I had the strength necessary to do it. While this experience was not the same as the crossover experiences I would have later in life, it set the stage for all that came after. My life changed overnight, never returning to the addictions that had gripped me for years.

At that same time, the voice spoke to me again, "After you are baptized, you need to stay strong until I come again. It will be hard, but it is very important that you do."

I was dumbstruck. I had a chance at redemption! I felt joy for the first time in a long time. I had direction. I had hope. Someone – not just someone, God! – actually believed in me. With all the mistakes I had made, I felt like I had lost the faith of everyone in my life. But somehow, the greatest of all was paying attention to me. It was almost like His belief in me finally gave me the chance to start believing in myself. He was giving me the attention that I so badly craved. I didn't want to mess it up. I knew I needed to do everything perfectly.

In fact, every day thereafter, I would literally lay down in supplication in the shower as a symbol of my nakedness before Him and offer my life up to Him even as Jesus had given His life for me. I would just lay there and cry. I literally pled with him that I might have the chance to die for Him someday. I didn't know at the time how hardship tends to find those who ask for it.

Thus, I was baptized at age twenty-one. After my baptism, others at church noticed my zealous religious conviction and obedience. I used to tell them that if they had seen what I had seen, they would do what I did. Where they believed, I had experience. I "knew." While I felt that God would mercifully forgive them because they did not know, I had the pressure in my heart and mind of fearing the loss of forgiveness if I even made one mistake, because I *knew*.

While I was still too young to see the parallels, I felt a very similar relationship with my Maker as I did with my earthly dad. In both relationships, I felt an impossibly high standard to be perfect in every detail. Only with God, I believed that there was no running away. I had to stay and face my problems or suffer an eternity of torment.

This desire to please God led me on a two-year religious mission in a foreign country. It was in the time preparing for my mission trip that I first heard the idea that we could see Jesus in this life. One of the books I read suggested that seeing Jesus in this life was not only possible, but it was the crowning event for a person who followed God with all their heart. Given the fear I had prior to my baptism and the need for validation I had from God, I put all of my hope into this idea. I prayed almost daily for this experience, that I could lay down my life for Jesus as he did for me, and that the day would come when he found me worthy of visiting. There were a few times when I felt an unbelievable love poured out in response to that prayer, and I believed my prayer would be granted.

After my mission, my desire to please God led me to get married and have children at a young age, and later to pursue a Ph.D. in bioengineering with an emphasis in entrepreneurship. I wanted to invent low-cost diagnostics for infectious disease to lower the cost of health care in the developing world. I also knew that reaching the people who needed it most would require significant innovations in the business model.

I spent the next three years traveling around the world, meeting with governments, donors, and investors. The response of one investor I was convinced would help us was typical of what I heard from others in the venture capital community, "That's an amazing idea! And I wish you the best of success... but with someone else's money. You see, our fund is charged with making the best return on investment. You can't get that in high-risk markets, especially where people can't afford to pay for products."

We ran out of money several times, but I was too committed to the vision to quit. Jenn, despite the young children we had at home, was just as adamant in supporting the vision. She believed in me completely and owned it with me to the point that it was not my vision alone, but ours together. In that way, she was my rock and would not have let me walk away even if I had wanted to. For her, quitting or giving up were never on the table.

One Christmas, we were driving back from my parents' place and stopped at a McDonald's to use the bathroom. A homeless man approached us asking if we could spare any change. When I turned him down, he yelled at me, accusing us of being fat and happy while neglecting the poor. I lost my temper for a moment and replied bitingly, "I haven't been paid in almost a year. My kids are in the car, crying because I don't have money to buy them any food. And the best present I can give them this year for Christmas is the news that we are getting kicked out of our house and have no place to live."

As hard as it was to lose our home, shutting down the company and moving out of the lab we had rented in South Carolina was even harder for me. The company was my baby and I knew it would succeed if we were just given the chance. At the time, I couldn't even understand the possibility of failure, so I just kept staring at the now empty lab in a state of disbelief. Hopes and dreams are the hardest thing to let go of. The deeper they are, the more painful it is when life takes a sudden change in direction.

What made it so much harder than just starting and failing a normal business was that the only reason I had the confidence to step out in such an impossible undertaking to begin with was that I felt God's assurance in my heart. I knew He was with me and would help me. I just couldn't understand why we had failed. It was impossible! God delivers those who trust in Him, doesn't He?

I felt like a sapling that can bend with the wind, but after being pushed and pushed beyond even its extreme flexibility, it simply snaps. How do you ever put the tree back together once it is broken? I remembered that feeling of snapping and thinking, *Even if He does deliver us now, it's too late. I can never recover from this. Something just broke that can never be repaired.*

Chapter 2

Visions of Glory

A few years later, I found some investors in Utah who considered lifting the world as part of the return on investment they were seeking. So, we relocated to give the idea a new start with a fresh perspective. What I didn't know at the time was how different the next puzzle piece was actually going to be from the picture I had of my life, or the circumstances that would lead to it. I was completely clueless what was happening in the culture around me in Utah at that moment. Specifically, there were a growing number of people who were claiming to have seen Jesus in near-death experiences and some of these visions were really shaking things up. Shortly after arriving in Utah, one of our friends approached me about one of the experiences she had read.

"I really think you should read this book, *Visions of Glory*," our friend Julie confided to me.

I just stared at her. I was already processing polite ways to refuse, but as she often did, she continued as if she didn't notice, "It's the story of a man here in Utah who had four near-death experiences and saw the events leading up to the return of Jesus."

Ordinarily, I was suspicious of anybody claiming to see Jesus that was not in the scriptures. In my brief stint with Hinduism before I was baptized, one of my trusted teachers claimed to have seen Jesus. His teachings were part of what I used to justify the life choices that led to my extreme fear of being cut off from God. When I was baptized, I decided he must have intentionally lied to me about his experience with Jesus, further amplifying my fear of being deceived. This left me with a deep aversion toward anyone else's experiences of seeing God that were not part of canonized scripture. I did not want to be deceived again. The thought that I might somehow be led astray and not make it back to live with God, or that I might disappoint Him in any way was unbearable. This was all the more true because my experiences with Him before and after my baptism led me to "know" He existed. In my mind, where much was given, much was required. Consequently, I felt I could not risk another offense with God. I had used up all of my second chances with my wild teenage experiences and with those I felt had misled me religiously before.

Further, if God ever did talk to people, I believed it would have to be a very holy person, like the prophets and apostles in the Bible. For some reason, I did not see the inconsistency between this belief and my own experience in hearing a voice before my baptism. Perhaps this loophole in my logic existed because I had not "seen" God. Or perhaps I justified it because the experience I had was uniquely mine, part of an internal compass that I trusted to guide me more than the experiences of others. The authority of internal experience seemed to outweigh every vestige of external authority, except for a possible trusted few designated by God. In other words, the only visions from others that I felt I could trust came from individuals like those in the Bible.

While I thought maybe on very rare occasions an ordinary person like me might have a private and sacred experience with God, I believed that it was very personal and needed to be kept private. To me, God was a God of order and would only allow his light to enter the world through holy prophets and apostles like those found in the Bible. That way disciples of Jesus knew who to trust; the sheep could have confidence in the shepherd who entered in through the door.[5] Therefore, God would only reveal Himself to an ordinary person if they had the spiritual discipline to not reveal what He shared with them. In my opinion at the time, the best sign that a vision or experience given to someone was not from God was if the person didn't have the integrity to

---

[5] "Verily, verily, I say unto you, He that entereth not by the door into the sheepfold, but climbeth up some other way, the same is a thief and a robber. But he that entereth in by the door is the shepherd of the sheep... and the sheep follow him: for they know his voice." (John 10:1-4)

keep it sacred and instead shared it with the whole world (e.g. by publishing a book).

As if reading my thoughts, she added emphatically, "I know I tell you about a lot of things, but I really feel that you're supposed to read this one."

It was true that Julie frequently came to Jenn and I with a lot of ideas that made me squirm for both religious and scientific reasons. She had healed herself from Chronic Fatigue Syndrome after making a pilgrimage to see a shaman in Russia and living on a diet of lemons and raw garlic. Possibly for that reason, she embraced a lot of alternative and scientifically untested ideas. She was used to me listening politely before finding a way to change the subject. But on this occasion, I actually felt she was right. As she spoke, I felt an expansion of light within my heart. I knew from experience that this was how God placed mile markers in my journey to help point the way I should go. Besides, it was a book. Was there really that much harm in reading it? If I didn't feel the light, I could always put it back down.

"Ok," I replied candidly. "I'll look into it."

A few days later, on my anniversary, I stopped at the book store to pick up a copy. I imagined I would just read a few pages and then take my wife out somewhere for dinner. I didn't realize that once I picked it up, I would not be able to put it back down. Much to my wife's chagrin, I devoured it in a single sitting. (In fairness, Jenn and I spent so much time romancing each other in the early years of our marriage, that there was less emphasis on special moments like anniversaries or birthdays – every day was special to us.)

While the book goes deep into visions of coming changes in Utah, it wasn't the apocalyptic scenarios that really gripped me. It was the man's encounters with Jesus. He described looking into Jesus's eyes and feeling a love deeper than anything he had ever known, a perfect love that healed him. In a description of his life-like vision, he said:

> *I was halfway up the walk... when I heard, 'Spencer.' The voice was familiar to me, and I turned around to see who had spoken my name. I was astonished to see Jesus... It felt to my soul as if I was seeing my most beloved friend for the first time after decades of absence... He smiled at me, and I dropped my briefcase and ran to Him. His arms engulfed me. I can't find words to explain how it felt to be embraced by Him... I felt His love for me radiating from Him. I knew by instinct that He knew everything about me, yet there was no sense of judgment... He again said, 'Spencer,' and for a moment I saw myself as He sees me and knew myself as He knows me... In that moment He spoke my name, I was given to see and feel the full meaning of my name to Him. It melted my heart and still does to this day every time I think of how He said my name. The love He bestowed upon me in that one word cannot be described in any mortal language.[6]*

My whole being lit up at the description. In my mind's eye, I could imagine being healed myself. That broken place inside of me would somehow be lifted, somehow be whole. The world would make sense once more. I never wanted anything with more of my being. Those words changed me. I felt hope.

Most Christians do not believe that people can see Jesus, although there has been a small change in sentiment following Colton Burpo's experience in *Heaven is for Real.* Even in my church, the possibility of seeing Jesus was believed, but treated like folklore. If it ever happened, it probably only happened to the highest ecclesiastical authority or to someone who was so holy that nothing could ever corrupt them again; it simply wasn't something that everyday people could aspire to.

For me, this was no deluded fancy. It was very real. It was something I not only believed with all my heart, but I desired it with every part of my being. It was the desire that was planted in

---

[6] Pontius, J. (2012) *Visions of Glory.* Springville, UT: Cedar Fort, Inc, pg 58-60.

my heart following my baptism leading up to my mission. This was the most tender secret in my heart that I confided to Jenn right before our marriage, the part of me that was larger than life. The whole of our marriage I continued to quietly harbor and cultivate it within me. In fact, there was nothing I wanted more. The feeling that enveloped my heart as I read these words was affirmation to me that God heard my prayer. Now, I prayed again with renewed faith that I might look into Jesus's eyes too, that I might find healing in my heart the way this man found in his.

Chapter 3

Dinner Guests

About two years later my company had grown from a seed into a full-fledged operation with outreach around the world. Our technology was ripening and we believed it had the potential to change the entire field of molecular diagnostics. I was optimistic that we would finally see the fruits of our labors.

Around that same time, I received a spiritual impression that change was coming. After the experiences leading up to my baptism at age twenty-one, sixteen years earlier, I had maintained a special connection with the other side. While I was given credit for each of my inventions, the ideas often came to me in prayer, sometimes without even looking for them.

One of my early spiritual mentors had taught me to keep a "sacred journal." That is, he showed me that my sensitivity to feeling God's presence would increase if I would take note of it and write the impressions when they came. I had been practicing this from almost the day I was baptized and it had indeed paid off. I credited all the opportunities I had received to following this still, small voice.

Jenn was a full participant with me in these directions as they came. We each believed that it was the role of a loving spouse to do all that was in our power to support each other in both receiving and following these whispers in our respective roles. It was a solid part of what made our marriage successful at the time.

Consequently, when I felt the characteristic peace in my heart that often preceded a message, I did not hesitate to listen. I did not question when it told me that my life was about to change or that I would be receiving an offer to sell the company soon. Nor did I question the fact that I should take that offer when it came, even if the offer was less than what I was expecting.

Just a few weeks later, my investors asked me if they could take control of the company. They told me that they would allow me to keep my stock and my salary; there would be no "sale" in a traditional sense. They would just take over. Effectively, I would be selling the company for free.

Years of perfectionist attitude in obedience to spiritual promptings took over. While my head said "No," my heart was oddly curious about what new adventure God had in store for me. Besides, I would have a salary that would set me free to follow the spiritual promptings within me wherever they would lead. I could only imagine what would be more important to God than impacting millions of his children in destitute nations.

While I didn't know it at the time, this paid, multi-year break in my life was important in so many far-reaching ways. Among other things, it set me free to have the experiences I have written about in this book. And it opened the way for my own deep healing.

Following the transfer of the company, Jenn and I moved into the mountains east of Park City. For the next several months, I spent a great deal of time in personal prayer and pondering. I wanted to understand what it was I was being asked to do next. It was starting to become clear that my idea of starting another biotech company was not consistent with what I was feeling from God. But what was I supposed to do?

The impressions from the other side increased to an unprecedented rate. I was spending an hour or more literally every morning writing the impressions that were coming to me. They flowed faster than I could write on almost every subject.

But this feeling of expansion left me feeling a little alienated from others in my religious community. It became clear that the majority were not having the experience I was having. So, what did this mean?

Even Jenn commented on this change. "I'm worried about you honey," she said. She had noticed a drop in my enthusiasm at church over the previous few months. "Ever since we moved, you haven't made any new friends. You don't seem to be enjoying the lessons in Sunday School anymore either. What can I do to help?"

The truth was, I was feeling less inclined to go. Something was changing inside of me that I couldn't quite put a finger on.

"I'm not sure," I responded. "Nothing anyone says at church seems to resonate with me anymore. There's only one person there who ever says anything that moves me."

She looked up quickly at that statement. "And who is that?"

"It's the older gentleman who sits near the back. You know the one that has a different understanding of scripture – that no one seems to hear?" She nodded for me to continue. "Well, for some reason what he says goes straight to my heart."

Being a scientist who preferred the rational behavior of the DNA I worked with on a lab bench to the erratic nature of interpersonal relationships, I sometimes failed to catch social cues around me. This was especially the case with my wife who was extremely extroverted and quick to fill any need she perceived. That's why later that night I was caught off guard when she approached me.

"Just so you know, we're having guests for dinner."

"Who?" I asked.

"I called that man's wife and the two of them are coming over in about a half hour."

"What?" I demanded. I disliked unexpected social situations. I had to make an effort to talk to other people when, as an introvert, I would have preferred to be resting in my own thoughts. That tendency was one of the reasons I had chosen lab work for my profession. "Why'd you invite them?"

"I was worried about you. And you need friends. Besides, you said that you like him."

"I said I resonated with what he said, not that I liked him," I protested. "I don't even know him! And besides, they're old enough to be our parents. What can we possibly talk about with them?"

There was no point in arguing with my wife though. The invitation had been sent and as much as I hated social situations, I was still a product of the South. I knew social graces, and it was impolite to retract an invitation once extended. I made the best of it and tried to put on pleasant airs when our guests arrived.

Our guests arrived promptly at the appointed hour. I made my way through the brief introductions and barely had time to think about my short list of polite conversation topics before our guest introduced his own topic.

"You may not know why you invited me here tonight, but there is only one reason you would have done so," he said.

This immediately caught my interest. This was not a standard "Let's talk about the weather," type of superficial conversation. But it was more than the words he offered, it was the way he said them. It was like time stopped for a moment and I could hear my heart beat. There was a familiar expansion of peace inside me that happened whenever I felt like God had something to communicate to me. It was this peace that truly caused me to sit up and pay attention.

He looked straight in my eyes and continued, "I prayed before I came over here and was told that you invited me here so that I could share an experience that happened to me a number of years ago, an experience that involved meeting Jesus. It's an experience I rarely share and only do so when directed."

My eyes grew wide. There was no way this man knew of the reaction I had while reading *Visions of Glory*. There was no way he knew about the seventeen years of prayers asking for that experience. And now here was someone standing in front of me, not only claiming to have had the experience, but also to have received instruction to specifically share it with me!

I was ready to cry. After so many years of believing it was possible, here was someone actually telling me that the whole reason we met was so they could share this experience! It was like God confirming to me that my prayers were heard.

The feeling inside me was electric. To me, this was not only a confirmation, but also an invitation. Somehow, I knew that God was waiting for me to have that experience too. The healing I was seeking was coming.

I stayed riveted throughout his whole account of meeting Jesus and what led up to it. But he wasn't done teaching me after sharing the story. He was just starting.

"Do you remember Jesus's parable of the ten virgins?" he asked.

I did. This parable was very familiar to me. There were ten virgins invited to a wedding feast. But the bridegroom was late. Five of the virgins were wise, preparing their lanterns with extra oil while the other five were foolish and did not. The foolish virgins were not prepared with their own light when the bridegroom came later and were unable to follow him to the wedding feast. Nor could they borrow light from others; each needed their own light.[7]

I nodded, indicating I remembered. He continued, "Virgins symbolize the pure in heart, the disciples of Jesus. The parable shows that half those who call themselves disciples will not have prepared for Jesus by learning to follow the light he has placed within them. Instead, they will try to rely on the light of others, listening to their words instead of cultivating their own connection with God."

Half was a big number – a number sure to make the faithful squirm. So far, though, he was still sharing insights I already had into the parable. I listened intently, sensing he was about to make his point, "But the real question is, do you know how many of the virgins were asleep when the bridegroom came?"

I had no idea. I had never thought to ask that question before. "Five?" I guessed. It was a reasonable assumption. Five of the virgins were wise, so maybe they were wise enough to stay awake?

"Ten," he answered. "All ten were asleep when the bridegroom came, including the wise virgins."

---

[7] Matthew 25:1-13

41

He paused while I searched my memory of the scriptures. He was right. The parable *did* say that all ten were sleeping when the bridegroom arrived. I nodded for him to continue.

He asked, "Do you know what this means?"

"No," I responded frankly, suddenly very curious.

He finished strong, the words entering directly into my being, "It means that none of those in the church will understand what Jesus intends to do when he comes. They will be 'asleep' as to true understanding of his teachings. Only a small number will be prepared to help the rest wake up when that time arrives."

I sat dumbfounded. The *entire* body of believers asleep? What could they possibly be missing from the scriptures? Was this why people in near-death experiences were seeing things differently than what religions were teaching? My heart raced as I had the next thought — and why is God telling me this now?

I had never heard someone speak this way before, but I felt the truth of it. It thrilled my soul as he continued to open the scriptures to my mind. These were the words that I had been starving for. I was famished, and in this chance dinner meeting, God had prepared a feast for me.

He interrupted the flow of thought to ask one more question, "One thing I need to know before I tell you more. Have you read *Visions of Glory*?"

Chapter 4

First Experience: Jesus and the State of No Fear

A few weeks after the dinner meeting, our dinner guests began introducing us to other people who had also seen Jesus, some of them in near-death experiences. One woman in particular had been through four near-death experiences and spoken with God in each one. I was a little surprised when she reached out to me in a phone call one day before I even knew who she was.

"Hi, my name is Judy," she said as if I should know who that was. I was accustomed to people calling me for work, so I assumed we must know each other from somewhere. Before I even had a chance to ask, she answered, "A mutual friend mentioned you to me. I'm supposed to work with you."

I was a little taken aback and slightly confused. I just received a phone call from someone I didn't know and the first thing they say is that they are supposed to work with me? "What do you mean?" I asked.

Judy replied without hesitation, "I'm not sure if you've heard my story yet, but I died in a plane crash a number of years ago."

Silence. This was not the kind of phone call I was expecting. But she had my attention. I waited for her to elaborate.

She continued, "Due to complications from injuries I had in the crash, I died several more times as well. Each time, I saw and was instructed by God. I'm supposed to work with you."

If I was confused before, I was all the more so now. "I'm still not understanding what you mean," I replied.

"Just come over. You'll see," she said.

I was in such a state of learning and excitement, that I simply did not question what she was saying. To be contacted by one more person who had seen God and was feeling directed to share something with me was just one more confirmation. I didn't have to know what was involved, I was going. As to Jenn, she shared in my wonder at all these new developments. She always believed that this was not only my purpose, but our purpose together. Whatever privilege I received belonged to both of us. She too could feel the proximity of something beautiful.

The day for our appointment arrived and I met Judy. She had very kind eyes and immediately took my hand. I wasn't sure what she was doing or why, but suddenly I felt very different. It felt like she was looking into my soul and reading everything that was there.

Her husband looked at me sympathetically while she was doing this. He explained, "Some people receive gifts when they are on the other side. They rarely talk about them because society and even their own families don't understand. But when Judy was on the other side, she received a gift to see into people's souls."

"Is that what she's doing with me right now?" I asked.

"Yes. She's looking to confirm the work she is supposed to do with you. What she's contemplating is not something she does very often and only does so when she feels directed by God. That's why she's looking for the confirmation."

"What is it that she's been told to do with me?" I wondered out loud.

Whether I expected an answer or not, he replied anyway, "She's been instructed to help you cross over."

That answer caught me off guard. I had no idea what he was talking about, but I was excited by the implications. "Cross over? What do you mean by that?"

"Remember when I told you that some people receive gifts on the other side?" he asked. "One of the more special gifts she received during her experiences was the gift to help people cross over to the other side without having to die to get there. That's the work she feels called to help you with."

My heart rate sped up. It was suddenly clear that I had not just been invited here to talk, but to be prepared for the experience I had been praying for during the last seventeen years.

Judy came out of her deep state and looked at me. "Yes, I'm supposed to help you cross over. You're supposed to return every week for the next several weeks while I teach you to relax the part of the mind that keeps us separated from the knowledge of God. That's the part that 'dies' in a near-death experience. You're supposed to keep coming back until you cross over. You are supposed to meet Jesus."

She also made another comment that struck a deep chord within me, "It's time to lay down your sword. You have been fighting your whole life. It has worn you out. It is time to let go of the fight and let God take over. It is time to rest."

How had she known what a burden I had been carrying for so many years? How had she seen that I truly had been in a state of chronic stress? Even just thinking about "laying down my sword," caused me to almost weep from relief. I could feel a huge release inside me. It was like all the tension that had been held there for years simply started to come undone.

At this point I was truly excited for every visit. I couldn't wait. Like a child right before Christmas, I was counting down the days and the hours before each conversation.

It actually wasn't until our third or fourth visit that things really started to heat up. This time was different than normal. When I walked through the door, I had a vision, or rather a feeling that was so intense that I could see it.

I saw that I held what looked like a tiny piece of her heart. I was supposed to give it back to her. The feeling was so intense I didn't even hesitate. I didn't question that this was possible or even how it could be done. I immediately moved my hand to place it over her heart.

All at once, I became conscious of what I was doing. I stopped with a little bit of shame. *What am I doing?* I thought. *I can't just put my hand on a woman's chest who isn't my wife!*

45

While I had not spoken my intention to her, she saw me start to move and then stop. She read my intention as though she had seen the very thing I had seen. She told me, "Jesus would do it. That is exactly where he puts his hand." She then grabbed my hand and placed it squarely over her heart.

No sooner had she done this than I felt a rushing of energy through my entire being in a way that I had never felt before. I also experienced a melding of the minds where our thoughts literally became one to the point I could not tell whether it was me or her who was thinking. The buzzing vibration in every cell in my being continued to increase.

This sensation was new to me. It was foreign. I felt pins and needles through my entire being in a way that caused my whole body to go numb. It made it difficult for me to stand or have any muscle control whatsoever. I couldn't even speak properly. It was like the current from an electric fence across my entire body, but instead of electricity flowing through me, it was divine love.

This feeling was an intensely joyful one, but owing to the intensity of it, it was also a little scary for me. I simply had no context for what was happening.

I explained to her what I was feeling and asked, "What is this?"

As she listened to my explanation, she became very excited. She said, "That's the feeling that comes right before you cross over."

She instructed me to lay down on the couch where she then took hold of my hand and used her particular gifts to help push me the rest of the way through to the other side. As I fell deeper and deeper into the intense love of God, I could hear her voice cutting through the fog, "Remember…"

The vision opened up with immense bliss. I felt like I could see all of the tingling molecules in my body. I could see the vastness of space in between the molecules that our world calls "matter." But that space was not empty. It was full of a glowing and beautiful light. There was a current running through all of it that was intensely joyful and equally intelligent.

I saw that all of these molecules were instructed by the light. They had a specific purpose to align themselves with the needs of my deeper being. By deeper being, I am referring to a part of ourselves that is deeper than the conscious mind, kind of like our spirit or soul. I saw with some surprise that because of this purpose, the molecules that made up my body were in fact obeying me perfectly. From that perspective, there was no disease, injury, or deficiency at all. All of the imperfections and the things I unconsciously resented about my body were actually showing up exactly the way I was asking them to on a very deep level.

In understanding this interconnection, I could see the resentment I poured forth on aspects of my body. For example, I resented the weakness in my back. In contrast to the strength I felt when I was younger, sometimes my spine would slip so badly that I was literally paralyzed on the floor. Instead of being able to do the heavy lifting in the home the way I felt a man should do, frequently Jenn had to do it on her own. I felt incapable of supporting her the way she really needed and wanted. I still remember Jenn taking me to the emergency room during one episode because my back had slipped badly enough that I could no longer breathe. In that instance, I had only been carrying a featherweight baby mattress. However, it was more than just physical aches and pains or even the way my body looked. There was also resentment toward mental and emotional issues such as the chronic stress and depression that I felt kept me from measuring up to God's love or being an adequate husband and father. My response to all these things had been to exercise more discipline, using unconscious resentment as a whip to put my mind and body back into shape.

In the light I was now in, I could see how misplaced this resentment was. How could I hate any aspect of my body when every molecule was so lovingly and faithfully obeying each thought of my heart? I saw how this resentment had the opposite effect that I desired. Through resentment or self-hatred of any type, I was cutting off these molecules from the divine love that was in all things, the very loving intelligence that would eventually bring me the healing and change I so badly craved. What my body needed instead of me cutting it off from the light by being upset with it was for me to open the flow of light by loving it.

Judy's voice continued to come to me, urging me deeper. Suddenly, I had a memory return to me of my life before this existence. It was so full of light and emotion that it was more real to me than any of the memories I had in this life at the time. In fact, it was almost like the past was in the present, and I was even then experiencing it – a memory that was playing outside of time.

It came as a sudden surge of emotion and comprehension accompanied by visual understanding. I saw myself sitting with Father and Jesus before this life in a heavenly state. We were laughing together. In that one moment, I was filled with such immense joy as to cause me to weep and weep.

All my life I had believed Jesus to be serious. He was holy. He mourned with those that mourned. The scriptures even talked about Jesus weeping, but laughing? This was not the image of God I had been expecting. He had the innocence of a little child. His laughter was the most healing and beautiful thing I could have ever hoped to hear or feel.

The sternness and rigidity that had been within me for most of my life began to crumble. God's laughter immediately began challenging and overcoming any of the paradigms that had gone into creating that rigidity. God was so much more than a being to be feared. Without any words being exchanged at all to this point, I intuitively knew that He was love itself, and that my relationship with Him was the most beautiful and wonderful thing in the world.

The description that I recorded in my journal later that night said:

I saw that in the beginning I was with God. I was next to him. We were friends, but friends is not the right word. We were in love. We were the most intimate and closest of family. I was one with him in his presence. I felt unification with all of creation, all that was and is and shall be.

There was so much joy and love that the very molecules inside me seemed to be on fire, as though the fabric of my soul would come apart at the seams. Most importantly, there was no fear. In fact, this was the first time in my life that I ever experienced a state without fear and the first time I realized just how much fear the human body unconsciously feels on a day-to-day basis. The contrast between this state and the chronic stress I had been carrying is indescribable. It was a release that my body and being had no prior context for.

However, this went far beyond the stress others might see in me into the unconscious stress that is inherent to the nature and structure of the human body. In later years, I came to understand that this unconscious stress was not specific to just me, but was part of the fabric veiling the experience of God from one moment to the next; it was a defining aspect of human existence in its perceived state of separation from God. I could see for me personally, it was like my brightest and supposedly stress-free moments, including my prior experiences with God, were experienced through the lens of a welder's helmet that I didn't even know I was wearing. I could have been next to the brightest star and still not felt the heat of it or perceived its brilliance except as a dim dot in my outer awareness.

Prior to this experience, I would not have thought of life as being particularly fearful. In fact, I only noticed fear in extreme, life-threatening moments. However, after experiencing the state of no fear, I realized my entire existence has been made out of fear. When I noticed fear before, what really happened is that I merely jumped from the normal unnoticed background of 99% fear to a slightly higher state of 99.9% fear. My body literally did not comprehend what it is like to be free from the torment of the unconscious fear creating the veil over human experience.

However, in this moment, I saw what exists when all fear is gone: love and the most beautiful states of unity with God. Divine love is the most beautiful and precious substance there is. This love was nothing like the rigid boundaries I felt with my dad growing up or even like the emotional dependency I felt with my mom. Although I believe I have some of the best parents this world has to offer, God's love was almost the opposite – a feeling I had never experienced in this way before. It was unconditional acceptance creating an unimaginable feeling of safety leading to the liberation of the innermost soul.

That love was not something I just felt. It also taught me, by showing me that the state of being in the presence of God was perfect love, which casts out all fear.[8] And I saw that if there were even the slightest possibility of judgment, there would be fear. Therefore, human understanding of judgment contradicts the unconditional and absolute love that exists in the presence of God. I remember my awe in the realization that came over my entire being all at once: *There is no judgment.*

This idea profoundly affected my religious views at the time. While there were beautiful aspects to my religion, so much of my understanding was built upon the idea of judgment. It was built on fear. The whole reason I had been baptized was because I was afraid of God's judgment, afraid to mess up even one more time. And in a moment, I realized that my entire understanding was founded on a principle that was not of God. Judgment does not come from God – it comes from us. It is our judgment we need to be saved from, not God's.

God is love.[9] All religious observation that is based on fear, whether individually or culturally, is not of God. It is not consistent with heaven. Nevertheless, when I saw from God's perspective, I no longer even feared the fear itself. I experienced no enmity with the way that humanity perceives religion. It is perfect. It is exactly the experience for which we came here, which

---

[8] "There is no fear in love; but perfect love casteth out fear" 1 John 4:18

[9] 1 John 4:16

includes the chance to be completely enveloped in truth from different perspectives.

Years later, I read hundreds of other near-death experiences searching for more understanding of what I had seen and felt. For the first time, I intentionally sought out the experiences of those from cultures other than my own; I no longer wanted to hide from the truth that did not conform to my own worldview. While not all found words to describe what they had felt, those from each culture expressed the same surprise at a love which was the opposite of what had been taught in their religions, specifically a love without judgment. It is people who need judgment to make sense of the world, not God.

As I began to truly understand that God is love, my entire way of looking at the world was changed. In fact, one of the common after effects of near-death experiences is that people who have experienced the divine love can no longer look on the world around them the same. Their sense of self and other becomes distorted. They love in a way that many people around them see as being naïve.

And so it is. After experiencing that love, I could not even look on extreme acts of humanity such as terrorism with the same degree of judgment that I used to. I could only see God's perfection in all things. Because I understood this principle: "There is no judgment." As soon as I understood that principle for myself, then I began to extend that same mercy and love to all those around me.

It was like an unspoken chain of logic. The divine love made me aware of a similar light in all things, experiences, and even people. Just like how the view of my body changed after seeing the light in it and its perfect obedience to the needs of my deeper being, so too did my view of the world. I knew that, just like with my body, the world around me was responding to the needs of my deeper being. God did not hate the way it enveloped and loved me, and neither did I.

In fact, it did not help to hate the world, the people, or anything else in my experience, no matter how bad it seemed.

Hate and any form of animosity simply cut off the flow of loving intelligence into those spaces that most needed love in order to heal. The scriptural instruction from Jesus to love[10] and forgive[11] was for my benefit, not His. Just like with the molecules in my body, at some level, it was all there for my growth and benefit. It was all love. Only, my body was not developed enough yet to see or experience it as love from moment to moment the way that God might. My growth into that higher perspective was largely dependent on my willingness to allow the knot of fear in my heart to release, to receive all things in a perfect state of trust and acceptance, like the innocence of a newborn in submitting to the ministrations of its parents.

The memory of being in God's presence lasted for what may have been less than a second. But in that flash of memory, I experienced something more tangible than almost anything I had experienced before in this life. In that moment, the way in which I perceived my life and the way I acted changed unalterably.

While that specific memory of Father and Jesus was short lived, the experience on the other side continued to open and to deepen. Next, a series of messengers came to me each asking me what it was that I wanted. My answer was the same again and again.

The first set of messengers felt like old friends, like family. It was more tender than a reunion with a long-lost childhood friend. I do not wish to mention their identities because it is not important to the message I received. In our world, who we know indicates our relative importance. But there, the names were not important, only the love I was experiencing from God, which the messengers' presence seemed to amplify. I believe each of us, once we are free from our burdens of fear, guilt, and shame, will

---

[10] "A new commandment I give unto you, That ye love one another; as I have loved you, that ye also love one another." John 13:34

[11] "Lord, how oft shall my brother sin against me, and I forgive him? Till seven times? Jesus saith unto him, I say not unto thee, Until seven times: but, until seventy times seven." Matthew 18:21-22

have the experience of being the center of God's attention. Whoever is there to support that process will be perfectly orchestrated for our joy.

As it was, I understood them to be the gatekeepers that were appointed for me to return to the presence of God. Perhaps because I expected judgment day before seeing God, I got it – but in a way that completely freed me from judgment. Rather than looking at all the negative, the messengers only brought out the positive in me in a way that I had never seen before. The process of my interview with them felt like less a requirement and more a point of joy, specifically because it magnified my joy in seeing my answers to their questions. I do not know that everyone who returns to God's presence is required to have the same meeting, but it was joyful for me to do so, and so it was offered at least in part because of the joy it brought me.

They made a point of asking me questions that I knew the answer to, which filled our hearts (i.e. both mine and the messengers) with joy. In my case, they made reference to promises I had made within my religion. They wanted to know if I understood the meaning of the promises and ordinances. These were not the answers I would have given in life, as though reciting doctrinal definitions from a book, but were the answers derived from the very experiences of my life. There was a level of heavenly pattern recognition that helped me to make sense of how the experiences in my life matched the symbolism in the promises I had made. It was almost like life was a grammar school in which every-day experiences formed the vocabulary that allowed me to communicate the understanding that had always been deep in my soul.

It was more than just being handed the answer key; I was the answer key. That is, I found that my life had been orchestrated such that each of the answers were contained in the experiences I had. It was not a matter of getting it "right" or "wrong" so much as unveiling the understanding etched into the very fabric of my soul acquired during the experiences themselves. This understanding gave me the capacity to qualify myself free from the opinions of others that held me down for so much of my life.

In other words, it was not God who judged me, but me. The joy in my judgment came from my own understanding that I had mastered the particular principles I came to learn – what I had learned was sufficient. This was not at all like shame-based judgment on earth so much as the joy of seeing something as it really is, like the degree of joy in seeing that a flower is red. The messengers helped me see past the judgments of this world to arrive at self-acceptance in what life itself helps us obtain. For the first time, I was not blind in my ability to gather the answers from the material of my life. The veil had been removed in this regard.

Each answer consisted of a short statement or phrase. However, each word was accompanied by layers of meaning and corresponding experiences from my lifetime from which the meaning was derived. The answers could be compared to a Facebook photo with many tags leading to other pages, each containing many other experiences. All the information is contained within the single photo, only in our linear time, you would need weeks or months to unpack it all. But there, it was understood with joy in an instant.

Once I had finished with the interview, they asked the question designed to uncover the joy that was truly in my heart, "What is wanted?" With the memory of the love of Father and of Jesus still burning within me, I knew clearly what it was I wanted. In fact, there was nothing else worth wanting. I responded plainly, "I want to be like Him. I want to feel the love I had with Him, but to feel it on earth." My words were filled with information far beyond just what was spoken. They carried the unspeakable emotion of my heart. The energy of those words contained with them the request to not only be restored to God's presence, but to help bring that love into the space of this world. It promised to give everything, to lay down all that I was in order to be part of that experience.

While I do not recall the exact words that were given in response to me in that moment, I do recall the feeling of heavenly enjoyment that burned within the messengers. They understood not only my words, but the fullness of the message as it was contained in the light. We could each see it for what it was and take joy in it. Their pleasure was distinctly tangible in a way that filled each of us with joy.

In the end, I was admitted into a new location that shone with a light brighter than the sun. In front of me was a brilliant fountain and temple. I wrote in my journal:

I was restored to His presence in the most beautiful building I have ever seen. It was covered with all manner of jewels and was beautiful such as I cannot imagine or describe. I saw the doors open and the inner hall and chamber that filled me with joy.

While I don't remember much of the specific details of what it looked like any more than what was written in my journal, I do remember how enraptured I became with even the smallest of details. A single drop of water from the fountain or small indentation in the wood seemed to contain an entire universe of meaning and joy beyond anything I had ever known. Like looking deeply into a person's eyes, what initially appears to be a single color is resolved into so many flecks of different colors, each layered on top of each other like an acrylic painting. Only, in this case, it was an acrylic painting where all the layers could be seen in three-dimensional space and where the colors were made of a living light, each telling a story about life and creation that caused my soul to thrill with utmost joy. The deeper that I looked, the more detail opened up to my eyes. I could have spent hours completely absorbed there just looking at the minutest of details without any loss of interest. But as it was, I was ushered on in my journey.

Inside the walls of the temple, I was greeted by another pair of messengers, one of whom had religious significance for me. I felt it a privilege to be in his presence and to be greeted by the warmth of his smile. Once again, I was asked what it was I wanted. I responded again with my desire to be filled with the love and light of Jesus Christ. As before, I felt such warmth in response from the messengers and I was sent into the inner portions of the temple. Although I had no recollection of being in the temple before, I walked with an inner knowing of exactly where to go. In fact, it did not even occur to me that it could be any other way.

Finally, I was admitted into God's presence. But it was unlike anything I might have imagined. The details of this event are very fuzzy for me. I have a hard time sorting out whether I was physically in His presence (i.e. as in front of a personage) or whether I was simply part of the light. Or, the more confusing alternative, both. I wrote in my journal:

> *I felt that love and intimacy that I had with Him in the beginning. I felt it and saw that there was nothing to be afraid of. I felt all pain come off from me. I felt the purpose for which I had been born.*

In the state that I was in when I wrote these journal entries, I was so filled with light, that there was no need to write the details. All of it was so clearly present as information behind the words that to say anything more would have detracted from my experience of it in that moment. It was not only unnecessary, it also felt limiting.

The understanding in that space continued with the role of all those who will be awakening in this heightened consciousness, there were many who found joy in bringing that light into this world the same as I did.

> *I saw that we were to bring a fullness of the light of Christ into the earth. There was so much light to be unveiled. It was to be heaven upon earth. I felt the light and love of Jesus Christ spread throughout me. I felt I could do anything. There were no limits. There was nothing to be afraid of. We knew only joy in God's presence and that joy was possible upon the earth.*

Even at this time, the process of going deeper into God's light and love in order to bring it back in fuller intensity into my body began to be planted in my mind:

I knew that I must allow this same light to enter my body. I must no longer see my body as the enemy, but as a loyal servant. Each molecule had faithfully served me. I should reward my body with that light which I had in the presence of God, exalting each molecule until I was changed before God. In this way, all sickness and disease should depart from before me and I should be restored to His presence to know in full. It was not my spirit that needed to know these things from the beginning, it was my body. That was why I needed to allow the light to enter my body until my body was glorified and exalted and was restored to all the memories that I have in spirit before God.

Years later, I briefly met Anita Moorjani, author of *Dying to Be Me*. Her near-death experience illustrates this idea perfectly. She had visible tumors all over her body and went into a coma as her organs shut down. Her doctors told her family that she had less than twenty-four hours to live. However, on the other side, she was shown that the reason she had cancer was that she had never learned to love herself. This love was not the kind of co-dependent love we imagine in romantic partnerships. Rather, it was a form of opening the heart in true acceptance of one's whole self that allows divine love to begin to circulate within us. In her case, just understanding that principle caused her to spontaneously awaken from her coma and completely heal from cancer within just a few weeks.

Before I was ready, I was called out of the vision and back into my body. I did not know it yet, but this experience was the reason I had met Judy. This was to be one of my last visits with my new friend.

Chapter 5

Re-Cognizing the World

When we see the world around us, we do so through the means of several sensory mechanisms, such as touch, sight, smell, and sound. Various parts of the brain then interpret those sensory inputs as pleasurable or painful and assign meaning to those experiences. The prefrontal cortex then creates a personal narrative of these experiences defining who we are in relation to the world around us.

The first time we have an experience, the neural connections, or circuitry, that tell us what to think about it have not been formed yet. The processing within our brain that defines our experience and who we are in the midst of it through the creation of new neural pathways is something we call "cognition." When we run into similar experiences in the future, the newly formed circuitry containing implicit and/or explicit memory of past experience is accessed through "recognition." This allows us to feel the same emotions all over again, strengthening the neural pathway. To "re-cognize" an event is to experience it again without the filter of past circuitry to inform us what it should be. Rather than repeating the same thoughts and emotions, we experience it with a brand-new slate, as if for the very first time.

Significant spiritual experiences can so alter our perception of reality that it is as if we are experiencing the world around us for the first time. Past circumstances no longer have the same meaning and have to be experienced through new eyes. Because we have not experienced them anew yet, we do not know just how different we have become. This process of discovering the changes within us over time is "re-cognizing" the world. In Christian language, this rewriting of our neural circuitry into a whole new persona is the deeper spiritual meaning behind being "born again." That was exactly what happened for me in my crossover experience with Judy.

This experience profoundly affected my sense of self in connection with God and others. For starters, I felt physically different. Even several hours after I returned to my body, it continued to vibrate and buzz all over with a highly euphoric, electric-like feeling. But emotionally, I was even more charged. I had seen what my heart had longed to see, and my heart was overflowing with joy and excitement in a way that was indescribable. I longed more than anything to share my experience with others, to tell them all that I had seen and heard.

However, I came from a culture that believed personal spiritual experiences were too sacred to be shared. So, I did not feel comfortable even sharing this event with my wife and children at that time. I kept the whole event tightly bottled up. It was the feeling of being a small child who knows the biggest and most exciting secret in the world. They are bursting from every seam wanting to be able to share that information. And so it was that I squirmed internally knowing something so joyful and yet feeling unable to share with another soul. It was not until years later that I encountered other cultures who helped me appreciate how valuable it can be to share these experiences in proper settings.

As far as my wife and children were concerned, daddy was just in an unusually good mood for a number of weeks following this event. And as I was on sabbatical so-to-speak from work, there was no real impact in my work life.

But the real impact of this experience in my life was far more subtle and longer-reaching in its nature. The love I had experienced in that heavenly state was incompatible with the fear-based understanding of God that I had internalized in my youth. I did not see it at the time, but this experience was already starting to unwind aspects of my personality, beliefs, and behavior that had defined me for many years.

Specifically, the seed of awareness had been planted to see the difference between love and fear-based motivation of any kind, especially in a religious setting. This subtle change within me was so complete that I did not even realize how different it was from the beliefs and traditions I had carried until I re-encountered them in religious settings and conversations over time.

The differences from my prior beliefs, when I became aware of them, were almost too small to notice. Each week, I would perceive something in someone's religious commentary that was inconsistent with what I had learned or seen. There would be a reference to God that to all those listening sounded Biblically accurate, but to me had undertones of fear that were incompatible with the love I had felt. This seed of awareness of the difference between fear and love-based behavior continued to grow within me until it laid the foundation for every experience that came after.

Part 2

How Heaven Is Made

Chapter 6

Second Experience: Physics of Heaven

The experience with Judy did nothing but increase my spiritual fervor. In my soul, my experience was an appetizer, a promise that I was about to break through the veil in deeper and more beautiful ways. It also left me hungering for more understanding surrounding the transition of the earth into a higher state. How was this to happen? What role did the scriptural destructions play?

In my heart, I believed completely that if I laid down my entire soul, the heavens would open and I would see Jesus in a way that was much deeper and more tangible than in my first crossover experience, in a way that confirmed my worth to Him and my unconditional acceptance into His kingdom. The only question I had was, "What can I do that will be big enough to constitute a complete sacrifice of my soul?" After all, in my quest to be ever more obedient, I had already experienced losing my income and my home. If that wasn't a complete sacrifice, then what was?

Perhaps, the difference between the obedience I had already shown and the obedience I believed would bring me into God's presence was merely a matter of timing through the change in my intention. For example, when I lost my home following a spiritual impression, my intention had been to help people in impoverished countries through developing diagnostics – not to see God. Perhaps that fundamental difference was the key, and I did not truly have the belief that my actions could call down that blessing before meeting others who had seen God.

However, in my mind's logic, I did not make that connection. Rather, since all my experiences in obedience were in the past, therefore, the test of my soul must still be in the future. And it had to be even harder than what I had already experienced. Because if what I had already done was enough, I would have already seen God. It never crossed my mind that perhaps those events were already more than enough – perhaps I was already more than enough. Perhaps all that was lacking was intent, or even just allowance.

The thoughts that all I had been through was not sufficient did little to dissipate the perfectionist stress that continued to pop up in my life. While, my experience with Judy had released a large amount of that stress in some areas of my life, in other areas it had increased. It was less that the stress disappeared from my life, and more that it simply morphed into a new area. Now, it came from the idea that I was so close to the finish line. Similar to how a runner who is exhausted will suddenly find new reserves of energy when they see the finish line, so too did I now pick up my pace.

As it was, my heart began to pray for that soul-level test, even if my mouth did not make those words. My heart was pleading for whatever was necessary to bring me into that beautiful place with my Maker. And the law that was then operating in my soul demanded the complete offering of my being. As so often happens, the Divine answers the prayers of our heart.

A few months after my experience with Judy, I was given my Abrahamic-like task. Abraham, through his willingness to sacrifice his only son, may have been a recognized symbol of the faith I needed in order to have the experiences I so badly yearned after, but my first answer to God's request for me was, "No." It did not matter how many signs or wonders He gave me, my answer did not change. In fact, I refused to even tell Jenn what it was I was supposed to do, so God showed her for me. Even after she came to me telling me what she saw and giving me her full support, I was still terrified to take a step forward into the unknown.

However, after a few weeks, I began to soften. Why did I pray at all, if not to yield to what was placed in my heart? I gave in and surrendered to the divine. I placed my fear-bound soul in the hands of God and let go, trusting for the best. After a morning of heart-felt prayer, I finally capitulated, "God, if this is what you truly want, then I will stop resisting. Just let me receive you fully in my being." What I did not know at the time is that this is one of the most powerful things we can do—complete and total surrender of what we think we know and are to the divine. My faith was still in the external form of my sacrifice and obedience, not yet realizing that the surrender of my being was more important by far.

Immediately, upon surrendering my heart, I began to feel a surge of energy moving through my body. This energy was joyful and felt healing. It opened my mind to where I began to sense events about the future of the earth. I saw these so clearly that I wanted to speak them out loud so that Jenn, who was nearby, could hear them. While I do not remember the specifics of what I said, I remember the joy of feeling into those events. These future events were not the catastrophes that I had been so worried about previously, but euphoric openings of the heavens for individuals and entire communities. If catastrophes were part of the world's transition, they were not what I was being shown; they were not the focus of my experience. The words kept pouring forth. I was speaking without thinking. It was just pure joy pouring out in deeper and deeper waves. As I spoke what I was seeing, the feeling intensified until I could no longer speak.

As I lay there feeling waves of bliss start to open in my being, I saw clearly so many events from my life and how each one had brought me to this point. Sitting at the edge of this unfolding experience, I saw that it was the culmination of everything that had happened. I was not only seeing my life through the lens of time, like a series of dominoes lined up in a precisely calculated sequence of cause and effect, but I also seemed to be feeling into other realities. I don't fully understand that feeling even at present. It was as if there were a Light inside searching for the solution to an exceedingly complex maze, and It was taking advantage of multiple processors all running in parallel through alternate realities. Now attention was being brought to rest on the one processor that was on the verge of the solution. I remember the distinct sense of excitement that filled my being as the words ran through my mind, *This is the one where it happens. This the one where I break through.* My mouth formed words that I did not consciously understand, instructing my being to bring in all of my light wherever it was scattered. I wanted to be fully present for what was about to happen. I felt the answers my being was seeking were right in front of me and about to open up in an unprecedented way.

By this time, the feeling inside me had progressed to a sensation similar to my first experience coming through the veil, although much more intense. It was not unlike taking hold of an electric fence. Although it was joyful, it was very powerful, like the pulsating vibration of divine electricity flowing through my being. I could feel every molecule in my body as though each had accelerated thousands of times.

This electric, pins-and-needles sensation was causing my whole body to go numb. I could not feel the borders of my body anymore. I distinctly recall the sensation of surprise when I could no longer feel my face or lips. I was simply an intense tingling that made it hard for me to distinguish my own body from the world around me.

I could not have imagined the feeling growing any stronger, but it did. It erupted in my belly like a supernova. The same tingling that was taking place all over my body was now in my belly, but hundreds of times stronger and faster.

There was nothing but a blissful awareness of this intense energy. As I surrendered any remaining resistance into that energy, it began to move. The erupting-supernova feeling started to ascend upward toward my heart. When it entered my heart, I suddenly became afraid. The tingling appeared to me to be physical. It was like my heart was palpitating thousands of times faster than it should. I had the thought that if this continued, my heart was going to explode.

At first my reaction was fear. I began to feel the fear of loss of everything and everyone that I loved. I saw my wife and children. I felt the pain of loss. But then, I thought, "If it is my time, then I accept." I determined to surrender with full trust in God.

In preparation for what was to follow, I told Jenn that I was closing my eyes. I was not sure what was going to happen next, but trusted that it would be ok. I told her I was going to go with

God and even if it took me several days to surface (i.e. I might look like I was dead or dying for several days), not to disturb me — what was happening was of God.

As soon as I closed my eyes and let go, my heart exploded. I was free from the normal constraints of the body, and I immediately came forth into the most beautiful light I have ever seen. I say "seen," but it is probably more appropriate to say "felt," because I was not seeing with my physical eyes. I was *feeling* this light and perceiving it with a sensation not unlike vision.

People from all cultures who see God spontaneously in visions and in near-death experiences often describe a light brighter than all comprehension. They describe God as thousands or even millions of times brighter than the sun. In the big bang, scientists speculate that the heat was so intense that the atoms that give off light in the sun by undergoing nuclear fusion would have literally melted; the nuclear forces that hold atoms together could not exist in the presence of such a high energetic vibration. I have pondered a joy so intense that one's body becomes bright enough that it has a molecular energy that could literally melt the sun.

The light I was experiencing in that moment felt like that – that the molecules that make up my body would have completely come apart in the intensity of the joy and love that was coursing through my being. I had the distinct impression that if my body had been with me, it would have died. I was weeping all over. Most notably, there was no judgment whatsoever. There was no fear. There was only this overwhelming love-joy in everything.

Understanding of almost every event in my life up to that point came flooding into me. It was like being connected to the internet of God where knowledge on every subject became instantaneously available. It was also like having an expanded processor that could process information on hundreds of different tangents in parallel. The information downloaded, was understood, and then all the tangential questions on each line of new information were immediately answered in the same fashion all in parallel in a single moment in time. While I remember the overwhelming joy of comprehension in the sensations that came with the flood of information, I only have traces of those memories left.

I saw with great joy every aspect of my life. Even the hardest and most difficult portions suddenly seemed perfect, as if everything had been according to a great and divine wisdom. There was a feeling of having arrived, of having graduated in some way. It felt like I was never going to have to suffer again and that whatever state I had just entered into was going to be available to me from that point on.

I would learn in coming months that there is no time or space in heaven the way we experience them on earth. Everything I saw about my life in the future was experienced as if it were already a reality in the present moment. There was no separation from the future and the experience I was having; consequently, I did not understand time in that state. I could not see that in earth time there may be months or years intervening before the actual occurrence. Specifically, with respect to the understanding that I would have no more suffering, I was unaware that I still had the biggest trials in my life to come. However, in this moment heaven allowed me the luxury of feeling that I would never lose that state again.

I'm not sure how long I sat in the light luxuriating in a feeling that has been described by others I know who have had near-death experiences as "an orgasm times a thousand," but after a time I saw a figure approaching me in white. On the other side, knowledge comes before you ask for it. I knew who it was before he had even arrived. I felt his energy immediately, even as he appeared in my sight.

This was the experience I had been waiting for most of my life. My whole being thrilled with light. Indeed, there was another explosion in my heart that took me as much higher than the joy I was experiencing only moments before as the original explosion had taken me from my mortal state. If I thought I had known bliss in the moments before, now I knew something far more intense. Like an amoeba in a single drop of water that suddenly feels the expanse of being placed into a bucket of water, then the wonder at being placed into the enormity of a pond, followed by the incomprehensible magnitude of an ocean, so too did my joy expand. This feeling was brighter than the previous experience in the way that the full moon is brighter than the stars.[12]

I wept and wept as I came into the presence of Jesus. He embraced me with more love and tenderness than anything I have ever known.

When I finally settled down enough to hear, he began to speak to me. He talked to me about my life and the events I had experienced. But his words were not the point. Rather, they were the trigger point for consciousness to then expand and experience lifetimes of understanding and expansion surrounding each word being articulated. It was experiential learning where to hear was to understand through becoming the information itself. Each word was an unfolding revelation on multiple layers of experience and understanding all of which took place without losing the rhythm of conversation.

There was no judgment whatsoever from Him. It was more like an unveiling of truth that liberated me from any self-judgment I might have had. It brought understanding to everything I had been through. It allowed me to see my life through his eyes, through the eyes of a love and wisdom beyond anything I could have comprehended before. Everything, even my biggest mistakes, had been perfect. Beyond perfect, I saw them as the key ingredient in the experience of unfolding salvation I was then receiving. They unfolded before my eyes in colors and descriptions beyond language, holiness unspeakable. Understanding this allowed me to let go and experience grace and love at a level I never could have imagined before.

---

[12] Using levels of light to symbolize the joy associated with increasing comprehensions and experiences of God in the hereafter, Paul said, "There is one glory of the sun, and another glory of the moon, and another glory of the stars." 1 Corinthians 15:41 In this instance, the symbol helps illustrate how much greater my joy was seeing Jesus.

He continued talking to me, showing me things that would shortly take place in my life. I saw people and circumstances in my life, many of which I do not choose to share here because they are still sacred to my heart. But I saw each in context with events leading up to the transition of the earth. As with the impressions I had immediately before my heart exploded, these events were curiously absent of any hints of destruction. Again, not to say that there were no catastrophic events, just in my field of vision, their existence or lack thereof was unimportant relative to the pure joy of what I saw unfolding upon the earth.

In fact, it did not even occur to me until several weeks afterward that I had not been shown any of the destructions I had been so worried about in my in-depth review of scripture and the near-death experiences of others. The idea of apocalyptic destruction had been so completely removed from my mind that it actually took someone asking me if I saw anything related to this to realize the change that had taken place in my perspective. I had no desire whatsoever to dwell on the negative; all I could see was the joy of what was to come.

Beyond personal details, what Jesus shared with me about the transition of the earth was more of an understanding related to consciousness and the mechanism by which the transition would occur. As he spoke, he showed me how all life was interconnected. There was a field of shared consciousness that extended beyond just people into animals, plants, and the earth itself. All of creation had its basis in this network. Specifically, I saw there was a shared field of beliefs, perspectives, and understandings common to humanity that was responsible for the way the world shows up and how we experience it. Most of these beliefs were operative well beneath the level of conscious awareness. These beliefs, when imprinted on the light that is in all things, acts like a sort of programming that shapes the light, creating the perceived limits in our mortal bodies and the conditions for our experience. This in turn constructs a sort of veil, obscuring the higher states from our awareness.

I saw that the way we perceive beliefs in the world is backward. We tend to take ownership of our beliefs, as if we alone were the authors, or as if our experiences originated the beliefs. The beliefs, in our understanding, are insubstantial and unrelated to anyone else. However, in the space I was in, I saw the beliefs almost like independent life forces that are responsible for creating the bodily experience of humanity, similar to how a web of computer programs dictates the limits of our online experience. That is, few of us are responsible for creating the programming in our online browsers that shape the way we experience the internet. Rather, we choose what to "download" that creates our internet experience for us. Most online users accept the browser offered on their computer almost without any awareness that there is another option. Our choice to blindly accept the program further contributes to its popularity along with the ongoing illusion that there is no other way to experience the internet. In this way, we do not create the programs that shape our online experience, but "opt-in" to the programs that create for us. It is only when we realize that the best programs are not always the ones that came preinstalled on the computer, or alternatively that we have the ability to write our own programs, that we stop being controlled by the web and start rewriting it for ourselves and others.

Our beliefs are like that web of programs. They are the programs of life itself dictating the height, the width, and the depth of our mortal experience. (They are the boundaries of life as we understand it and the force that is responsible for creating the appearance of separation from God.) Just like with the internet, the beliefs exist independently of any individual, and yet depend on humanity as a whole being plugged into them for their survival and evolution. They dictate the strengths and weaknesses of our bodies, which then create our individual experiences that reinforce our acceptance of the web of beliefs as reality. This is a form of self-perpetuating, circular logic designed to prevent humanity from awakening prematurely. We simply do not see the force behind the development of the attitudes and understandings we arrive at or how those understandings are limiting our potential experience in this life.

The purpose in the blinding of humanity to begin with was not directly apparent to me. That is, I could not understand it from a mortal cause-and-effect type of logic. Rather, I simply saw the joy, the holiness, and the bliss that erupted in connection with our mortal experience, and I understood that it simply was that way. There was no need to ask the question why, because it just was. It just made sense. I saw that the joy of the unveiling of the heavens in the eyes of all who were upon the earth in that day was made more brilliant because of our formerly blinded state. Similar to how a surprise party is all the more exhilarating when the secret is kept until the last moment when everyone jumps out yelling, "Surprise!" Only, in this instance, it was not an intellectual secret, but a secret of having our hearts covered from unimaginable love, acceptance, healing, and joy.

In the experiential vision Jesus was communicating to me, I saw that the timing of that "surprise party" was not set the way we set a date on a calendar. Rather, it was dependent on shifts in human consciousness. It was an event that we were co-creating with God through the way we interact with the programs inside of our bodies and the field of human consciousness. Therefore, the exact day and time were not set until it arrived, because we were still changing events through our faith.

There was a connection between our individual awakening from that web of programming and the manifestation of an external joy that exceeds all comprehension upon the earth. The very programs which limited our current perception of heaven also limited our faith to receive and allow the experience of heaven on earth in the present moment. Those programs locked us into a semi-permanent cycle of negative creation, reinforcing limiting belief, which then reinforced experience. The programs had to be penetrated in a deep and transformational way. I understood that the type of experience I was then having with Jesus was an example of experiencing joy and light in a way that unplugs the body from the web of beliefs. Just having the experience would dissolve some of the programs that were inside of me; in fact, it was impossible for it to do otherwise. The same way that discovering your parents placing gifts around the tree on Christmas morning would start dissolving belief around Santa, so too did intimately experiencing God in any degree start dissolving the veil and the limitations of the mortal body.

I also saw how the softening of subconscious limiting beliefs within an individual affected the entire field of interconnected consciousness that went into creating our collective veil. A single person resolving what seemed to be their personal inner trauma could help shift perspectives for all of humanity. It was like we all suffered from the same inner knot of subconscious programs. To loosen the knot that binds you also loosens the knot that binds every other person.

Therefore, in order for the earth to rise up, there needed to be a shift in global consciousness. I saw that there were people all over the earth who would begin to penetrate the veil created by that consciousness, thereby connecting to the heavenly state of joy and bringing it into their bodies. I understand now that those individuals were like seeds sewn in a variety of different faiths and backgrounds with the purpose of elevating the whole. It was not only Christian consciousness that needed to be raised, but all branches of understanding and experiencing God wherever they were found in the world. The individuals Jesus showed me in my personal life were just a few of that number. By virtue of our interactions with each other, we would help each other further release the limits of programming within the body that create the veil.

All of those who had entered the world with a similar purpose appeared to me as so many lights across the surface of the earth. Some were brighter than others. I understood that each of these were experiencing aspects of the Divine in different degrees. These individuals were almost without number. There was divine wisdom behind the precise timing of who was present on the earth now and who was yet to come. Each had a role to play in loosening the knot that bound the consciousness of the human family. Each had come to loosen the knot associated with their particular culture, family, and belief system. As each released the deepest beliefs in their respective cultures and socioeconomic circumstances, it affected the entire network of programs giving rise to the matter in this world and our experience of it. This in turn caused the vibration of the earth itself to rise, leading to a raising of the vibration of everyone still on the earth.

I understood that every individual who penetrated the veil of limiting belief separating us from God loosened the knot, making it easier for the next person. Similar to how colonial explorers discovered a path, which was subsequently followed by pioneers, railroads, cars, and finally planes, so too does every person who breaks through the veil make the path easier for the next. Every person who penetrates that space sends ripples throughout the whole network of beliefs forming the veil, challenging its structural integrity. Once a critical threshold is reached, the whole network collapses and all who are still present on the earth will emerge into heavenly space in a single euphoric moment. Just like how popcorn starts to pop one kernel at a time, but suddenly a critical heat is reached and the whole bag begins to explode, so too would the hearts of those on the earth begin to burst with understanding and heavenly joy.

I understood that this whole process was the faith spoken of in scripture that was to precede the miracle. Only I saw this type of faith was not the one commonly practiced in the religions of the world; the emphasis was not on self-righteous obedience and sacrifice to external law. Heaven had never been brought down to earth through all the sacrifice and obedience in thousands of years. Rather, the type of faith that was responsible for changing the world we live in was the faith born of a complete transformation of consciousness. It was the collective faith that came from thousands or even hundreds of thousands of individuals penetrating the veil of programming that separates us from the moment-to-moment experience of the Divine. It was the faith that comes from the rewriting of our programs, including our religious programs, in the face of the actual experience of God. The new programs written from the experience of God then sent out a new instruction into the light, bringing back a new reality. This is similar to how the image in the mirror does not change until we do. It is the change deep within us that is reflected in the world around us.]

I saw that for this process to be accelerated to the point that the earth could receive the revelation that Jesus desired to give, there needed to be a few people who went deeper into the heavenly space and brought back a near fullness of that light into their mortal bodies. I was not given a number, only the understanding that a smaller subset of those penetrating the veil would find joy in going deeper and deeper. Effectively, these people would raise their vibration so high that it would pull the whole earth with them and all those who were on the face of it, similar to how just one or two people with phenomenal scores on a test raise the average of the whole class. These individuals along with all who penetrated the veil in any degree, were the leavening Jesus spoke of that could raise the whole. It only took a few to alter the course of transition.

The transition of the earth did not need to be traumatic. It could be joyful. Even if some few participants still chose to create drama, the rest of us did not have to participate in it. We could choose to "unplug" from those programs. We were not victims; we could choose to create our own path of transition. In fact, I was instructed in later months to no longer use my faith to fuel apocalyptic scenarios. Rather, I was to put all of my attention and awareness into joyful transition for both myself and as many in the world as were open to receive it. My question for you is how might it affect your life and the world as a whole if each of us unplugged from those negative programs too? Whether in the form of conspiracy theories, the nightly news, apocalyptic scripture, or other doomsday beliefs, what programs are you powering through your attention and heart-felt belief? I invite you to unplug from these now and start pondering what you would like to create instead.

I saw the magnitude of the revelation that Jesus desires to give. It was far too large to be understood by the limited spiritual awareness that most people now have upon the earth. We understand through words and through the filter of our experience, which filter is one of fear, guilt, and shame. I saw that it was impossible for him to communicate his revelation within the bounds of our language defined through mortal experience. Without a change in our ability to hear on all layers of our being in a way similar to what I was then doing, his coming would be wasted. This hearing was experiential love and bliss beyond measure.

As I contemplated the revelation Jesus wants to give, I saw the explosion of the hearts of so many countless people around the world, each coming into a state of joy, love, and bliss beyond comprehension – to the point of overwhelming tears of gratitude. The joy of those explosions were contributing to all others around them exploding in virtually the same moment. I saw that there were some few who had become so clear from the programs of the earth that they not only experienced their own joy, which was astronomical, but the joy of all those around them too. It was like an exponential reaction, where they could feel the eruption in others' hearts, which then magnified their own to the point of a whole new explosion, a whole new state of joy beyond comprehension. I felt the desire to be among those who could feel the joy of the whole earth, among those who went deeper and deeper into divine space. I also felt the open invitation. It did not feel to me like God was placing limits upon anyone. Rather, the limits were simply the desires in our own hearts.

I know at this point that much of what people see in near-death experiences and related visions is symbolic. We see it as literal, but do not understand that the heavens communicate through symbols. Our mortal minds try to fit the heavenly communication back into a form that we can understand and relate to. We try to take that which is beautiful and cannot be contained in our earthly words and put it into a box so that we can understand it and communicate it to others.

In talking about the revelation or return of Jesus, I realize it does not matter if that return is physical in the way that much of Christianity expects it or if it is symbolic of a revelation of Christ consciousness the way that New Age proponents speak of it. In my heart, I found joy in the idea that Jesus would personally come. It was part of my heaven. And that idea was the key to unlocking the joy I was then experiencing in my conversation with Jesus and the understanding that was unfolding upon me. However, whether Christ is to return physically or symbolically, that joy is beyond measure. And in either event the revelation cannot be given without a people whose consciousness has raised to the point that they can receive it. For the revelation cannot come with the words that humankind speaks. It is a revelation that speaks at the level of the heart.

All this time, I continued to receive downloads through the heavenly internet that searched out dozens of tangents on every word spoken and brought the full understanding into my being without interrupting the conversation. There was far more communicated that was not spoken than in what was spoken. Some questions he did answer directly with the words of his mouth.

As I pondered the changes to come, I was overwhelmed with joy. But for the first time I began to ponder the earthly reality of how this experience would affect my life. I felt limited in my ability to act on what I felt I was being given. I saw the bounds of religious and societal authority that I still respected deeply. I had made promises to God to stay subservient. So, my heart expressed the question already knowing that there was an answer in the love and intelligence that enveloped me, *What do I do with this information? How do I reconcile what I am seeing with the promises I have made?* Without even having to ask, Jesus saw the questions in my heart and spoke to them.

He told me he was changing my relationship to the world around me and its authority. Specifically, he spoke to me of promises I had made to him at the time of my baptism and later in the temple. He helped me to see their purpose and fulfillment in my life. He then symbolically took those promises from off of me by removing my clothing and placed a robe of radiant light upon me which he said would always be with me. I was under a new relationship with God in which I was to learn from direct connection with my Heavenly Father. I was to follow those things He put in my heart and no longer put others between us.

79

Jesus knew the effect this change in relationship would have on the fears in my inactive body when I returned to the world. While I felt nothing but joy in what he was showing me, my deepest fear had been that I might somehow hurt another person. I especially feared that in my desire to help, I would somehow be misunderstood. Specifically, I feared that the joy I was being exposed to in heavenly visions would disrupt the joy that those I loved took in their religious life. Further, I valued and took joy in many of their beliefs. How could I balance my joy in heavenly expansion with the need those around me had for stability and structure in what they knew? How could I balance it with my own need for stability? I feared I did not have the wisdom or experience necessary to balance these seemingly opposite objectives. I did not feel like any choice I made could possibly satisfy both.

Addressing the potential for fear and hurt in my body, Jesus then showed me the ongoing role and purpose of my religion in the world. It was beautiful, and I rejoiced in it. I saw their contribution in lifting people with a certain narrative and subset of desires in preparation for the revelation Jesus would bring. He also showed me how my own path would differ from theirs, at least for a time. It wasn't that I was prohibited from still participating with them or even that they would necessarily reject me. It is just that while I also desired to serve God, my understanding in how to do so and what that meant would lead me to interact differently with those around me. I would no longer "fit in." I saw that as I continued to have experiences with heaven, that divide in understanding would increase. And I did not want to disrupt the ordered and systematic beauty in their journey just because I was having a different experience. I did not want to disrupt their beliefs, and Jesus was showing me that I did not have to. There was a better way. I saw that my contribution would be most joyful among those who had an inner narrative similar to my own, not in disrupting the perspective of those who found joy in their existing narrative.

In the state that I was in, this potential change in relationship with those in my religion was not sad in the least. It made sense;

it answered the unasked questions of my heart. Everything Jesus showed me continued to expand my heart and fill me with a new kind of hope and joy. In fact, never at any time had I felt more joy in my being than in this moment.

As our conversation on the transition of the earth drew to a close, my heart turned to another question. It was my belief that when Jesus came to me that he would also lead me into the presence of God. My heart now trembled with increasing excitement like a child on Christmas morning as I remembered that belief. Jesus, again reading the joy in my heart, asked me, "Would you like me to take you into the presence of Father? He would like to see you."

My answer was given without words. No sooner thought, than there was a third explosion in my heart as we came through another veil. And as the glory of the sun exceeds that of the moon, so too did this joy exceed all of the joy and love I had felt until that moment.[13] Jesus led me into the presence of the being I knew as my Heavenly Father.

Some Christians feel that Jesus is the same as God the Father. In this instance, I saw them as two separate beings. In that state, I remembered Father as though I had known him forever. That relationship was not formal or stoic the way we learn in prayer, but it was loving and familial beyond belief. I crumbled in that love which, if it were possible, exceeded Jesus's own love for me. He was not the stern man I once believed Him to be. I did not need intercession with Him. Rather, He was the very Love that Jesus embodied. He embraced me with as much tenderness, if not more tenderness, than Jesus had done. I thought surely my being would come undone as a result of this joy. Again, I found myself weeping uncontrollably.

---

[13] As before with coming into the presence of Jesus, Paul's symbol of the different glories of comprehension and experience in the hereafter helps illustrate my increasing levels of joy, "There is one glory of the sun, and another glory of the moon, and another glory of the stars." 1 Corinthians 15:41

Father proceeded to show me the same things Jesus had shown me. Only, it did not feel like a repetition. From His lips, it felt like a new-and-everlasting revelation of joy. I would have listened to Him forever. His revelation also seemed to expand my former understanding, giving me deeper insights into what Jesus had discussed with me. He also confirmed Jesus's words to me with respect to my new relationship with Him. I was no longer to place others between me and my experience of learning through His love.

While we were talking, I also saw that there were several gifts brought to Father. I understood that they were my gifts to Him – not in the way a servant gives to a master, but in the way two people who share a common vision joyfully give gifts that serve the greater purpose. I was one in my joy with Him and of my absolute trust of what was and would be. These gifts were the particular lessons I had come into mortality to learn. These lessons were not just my successes, but they, even and especially, included my failures. They were the unique experiences and understandings gained through my individual trials and hardships. He received them with great joy and told me my process was complete. I had finished the first part of what I came to do and my old life was over.

I understood that each one of us has a uniquely crafted set of circumstances that gives us the capacity to extract a limited perspective on truth in isolation from a fullness of God's love. Every person on earth, both those we consider good and bad, occupies a unique kingdom of perception of truth. The perceptions they are born with and encounter throughout their life allow them to experience perspectives of truth in a way that no other person ever has or will. Even the person on the street lives according to the limited principles of truth that have been discovered by their being. For some reason, these lessons and experiences were important to Father, so much so that I perceived them as gifts to Him by fully living and exploring my personal perspectives on truth in mortality.

I understood that my gifts to Him were the contribution of my life and that each person who comes to earth makes a similar contribution to God. While I did not ask about all the details, the unique circumstances and limiting beliefs that each of us were born into seemed like a gift from God so that we could have experiences that would emphasize different perspectives of truth. We saw these experiences as a means to increase not only our own comprehension, but the understanding of the whole. In the heavenly state, the joy of each one of us contributes to the joy of all of us. If it were possible for God to grow bigger in heavenly ecstasy, then we were part of that process, and we were joint-heirs to all that He had. Everything we learn in this life, every hardship we undergo, is consecrated not only to God, but to the entire family of God. It was in service to the whole family of God that we descended, that is that we took on bodies. No matter how bad our circumstances may seem at times, we were the ones to joyfully choose them before this life.

As the gifts were transferred to Father, I understood that my life purpose was fulfilled. He told me that my process was "100% complete." However, rather than choosing to pass into the next life as was customary, I was ready for my next assignment. I think it was already understood that I would not choose to stay with Him, as if that decision had already been made before I even came into this life. In fact, it did not even occur to me that I could have stayed in the heavenly presence. There were new perspectives to be had that I wanted to offer to Father through continued mortal experience. It was time to begin phase two of my journey. The revelation and understanding I was then experiencing in His presence would provide a whole new context for mortal perspective on truth. The old me was dead or possibly complete. Dead is the wrong word, because it was never in the cards for me to stay in heaven after finishing my first objective. I believe I was always meant to return to life under new circumstances and with new purpose. While I understood that I had embraced a new assignment, I had no idea what those experiences would be. It did not even occur to me to ask. There was no question, it simply was. Later I was to learn that my assignment was nothing at all like what I had experienced before, that is an ongoing feeling of something that had to be done. Rather, it was more like the witnessing of the unfolding of heavenly joy in earthly space – not something I "had" to do, but something I was allowed to experience. For the time being, however, I still imagined that God had other "tasks" for me, not realizing that joy in being was the task itself.

As this conversation came to an end, I again trembled with anticipation. Just as it had been my belief that Jesus would lead me into the presence of Father, I also had a belief that Father would lead me deeper and show me all things. And as happened with Jesus, Father knew the thought as it arose, almost as if the very thought in my heart were orchestrated by God as part of a grand, divine timing. He said to me, "There is someone else who would like to see you. Would you like me to take you?" Again, the answer of joy happened without words. At His very suggestion, I experienced one more explosion of the heart, coming through another veil into a whole new state of joy and bliss.

Christian culture sometimes acknowledges the presence of Jesus and of God as separate beings. However, few if any, ever discuss the female element of God. In my experience, I was led into the presence of someone else who I knew to be the most wonderful person in my life—my Heavenly Mother.

As much love and as much joy as I felt in the presence of Jesus and then of Father, the love from Mother was completely unique and that much more intense. Never had I felt such a perfect and complete love as I did in the embrace from Mother. Just as in the biblical account of the creation the earth was not complete until God made Eve, so too was my experience of heaven incomplete until it had been crowned with the presence of Mother. It was Mother who made heaven perfect. I was finally whole, complete. I knew I needed nothing else.

My visit with Mother did not last long in earth time. That is, there was not a sequence of events or words exchanged. However, the visit was long enough for me to feel a fullness of love and joy in that moment. It lasted long enough for me to know what completeness felt like. I do not recall exchanging any words with Her – just Her embrace, which felt like eternity.

As we left Mother's presence, my heart was full. I do not recall any other questions or desires. My former desire to be shown all things had been placated, forgotten even. However, Father seemed determined to shower me with joy. "Would you like a tour of heaven?" He offered.

My answer was immediate. Like a child who quickly turns from the best experience of their life to a whole new joy, so too was I ready to go play with Father. However, our tour of heaven was not like the experiences of others who have visited and described it. I was not shown buildings or places or people. Rather, being a scientist, God knew that my heart desired something that not even I would have been able to articulate. More than all those other things, my inner being wanted to understand the physics of heaven. Specifically, how did it work? What was the underlying principle that allowed joy to expand for eternity and to never get old? So, this is what he showed me.

He unveiled to my eyes the light that is in all things and through all things. While people in visions of God frequently have differing experiences, the one thing that seems to remain the same with them all is the light. People often describe the light as shining *through* things rather than on them. Some describe the light as being loving and intelligent. It was this light that He showed me. He did not show me where the light comes from, nor did I think to ask – I was too absorbed in the experience.

I saw that it was indeed in all things. It permeated everything. It was in all of space. It was in me. It was in God. At some level that is hard to explain, it was God.

I saw that whatever we put into the light by virtue of the deep beliefs of our heart was returned unto us even as we sent it out. This then was the secret of the ever-expanding nature of the joy and love in heaven—by planting in our hearts that there was more, the light would return it unto us. We did not even have to know how it would happen, all that we had to know was that it would – because that was how the light worked.

This teaching was experiential. As God spoke to me, his words went deep into my heart. Even as they went into my heart,

I saw them go into the light. And then, I felt the light increase in intensity, bringing back even greater love and joy to me. It was like coming through a whole new veil, experiencing a whole new explosion of bliss and joy bringing me to my knees as though I were experiencing it for the first time. The joy was all the greater in seeing the connection between what was in my heart and what was returned to me in the light. This was truly a real-time experience. My joy was in the experience as much as the teaching. This then was the physics of heaven: heaven exists and expands in infinite joy, because of the interaction of our inner-most desires with the light that comprises all things.

God also showed me that this principle applied to the creations in my life. Although at that time I had not yet been fully exposed to the ideas of manifestation, he was teaching me these principles. He showed me a picture of my life. It looked like a heavenly painting in multiple dimensions across time and space. I saw the beautiful colors and shapes in it. I also saw parts of the creation where the light was not yet shining. He showed me how to bring light into the painting to increase the joy of the creation. Through these symbols, he was preparing me to see and recognize many principles of manifestation that I would run into over the coming years.

Some people run into difficulties understanding manifestation when they have received instruction to "pray." What they need to understand is that manifestation is prayer, just prayer with power. In our society, the word prayer has come to have a meaning for many people which is watered down and restricted. It has come to mean the recitation of a series of words in which there is rarely any faith or power. As an example, one of the first prayers I ever offered was in sixth grade for my granddad who had just been diagnosed with a tumor the size of a football in his stomach. In those days, people did not recover from that type of cancer. He was told to go home and enjoy what remained of his life. However, I believed that God could intervene. I knelt down to pray in the privacy of my own room and tried to recite the Lord's prayer as Jesus taught in the New Testament.[14] However, the words felt awkward and empty. I knew I needed to find a way to express what I needed, so I abandoned the recitation of words and spoke as a child does from my heart. A few days later, my granddad received news there was a clinical trial for a new type of cancer treatment. He was accepted into the trial and his cancer was completely cured.

Manifestation, like my prayer in sixth grade, is the use of power through words, images, and emotions in order to pray. It is prayer truly connected to the expansive feeling of our hearts with the faith to then let completely go rather than a sequence of empty words. Further, instead of praying to humankind's idea of an angry or stingy God who might decline a prayer, it is a prayer that is done with an understanding of the light that is in all things and our relationship to that light. God is not jealous of our use of the light or our connection to it. What few people understand in their reverence for the external God, and I was one of those, is that it is the role of the external God to reveal the internal god. Like a true mentor, the external God's role is not to captivate you in some state that is eternally below or beneath him, but rather to liberate you by revealing to you the light that makes him God that is in us as well. Or in other words, to reveal to us what it truly means that we are created in his image. There is nothing that gives the external God more joy than to reveal the internal god to those who have the faith to receive it that they might remember their power to create and start using it to bring about great good upon the earth. To the extent that we begin to wake up in the realization that we are created in His image, He takes immense joy in what we create.

It has been my experience that there are two levels of faith, one of action and the other of power. Faith as a principle of action is what is used in the majority of religions and in the world at large. It is the attempt to use our hands and our actions to control the world around us. That control might be in our efforts to obtain

---

[14] Matthew 6:9-13

jobs, houses, relationships or other external factors. It can also be in the attempt to control our internal world through our thoughts and/or emotions. In this way, both the secular and religious symbolically use their hands as matter to exert that control and physically make things happen, like using a hammer and nails to build a house.

Faith as a principle of power, in contrast, is the power by which God works. He did not use a hammer and nails to organize the earth. Rather, He put the words or desire into His heart and the light brought back to Him what He spoke even as it was spoken. Rather than physically building the earth, He watched as the elements responded to his loving awareness. The light returned to Him the desires of His heart.

Faith is not only a mechanism of power in God, but also in humankind who were created in the image of God. Manifestation is the use of faith as a principle of power to create in spirit, or in our hearts, and to allow the light to bring our creation back to us. Denying that we create does not change the fact that we do create and that most of what we face in our lives are the unconscious creations stemming from subconscious programs. Therefore, manifestation is not the act of hijacking power from God, but rather remembering the power of God already within us and taking back conscious control of that creation rather than deferring it to our subconscious autopilot programs. It is to use prayer as it was originally meant to be used: with power and intention.

Manifesting was as simple as what Father showed me. There really are no steps, but if you had to summarize, just *feel* the emotion of what it is you are creating. For example, imagine what it would feel like to have a partner who actually respected you. Or imagine what it would feel like to be free from the worry of paying that bill. You know when you have hit the feeling in the right space when it causes your heart to expand. It begins to be delicious to you. It enlightens your mind. I have found in my own manifesting that the reason I manifest is more for the healing I experience when I allow those emotions into my heart. It feels like the return of blood flow, a sudden release of emotion that sometimes leaves me crying tears of gratitude. The feeling can be so real that there is no longer any need or desire for what was being manifested. This naturally leads to the second step: letting go. If you have experienced the emotion of what you are manifesting fully and completely, letting go is easy. There is no more need. The faith of generations past that clings to what we want is actually inhibitory to how the laws of heaven work. It is the opposite of faith, which is more about surrender and letting go of the outcome.

It may seem impossible for the body to feel an emotion for an experience that it has never had. But it is easier than you might think. Just imagine for a moment the day of your first heart break. Can you still feel the sadness? Imagine the happiest day of your life. Can you still feel the warmth in your heart? You are creating emotions all the time without even knowing you are doing it. Every memory, every thought is generating emotions that have little to nothing to do with the present moment. Most of us simply haven't realized that we can intentionally bring emotions into our heart, or that when we do so, life has a way of mirroring back to us what we just put into our heart.

I have used this hundreds of times (although like many people, I still have areas of my life that sometimes feel stubborn to change, or that change in ways that are hard for me to process). For example, I had a $15,000 bill that I was dreading. I went into meditation (meditation helps put the self-critical part of the mind to sleep making it easier to feel new emotion) and felt what it would be like to not have to worry about the bill. A little while after the meditation, I received a phone call telling me that due to some mix up in the billing system, the bill had been paid; I didn't need to worry about it. In another instance, I wanted to know what it would feel like to have the stock in my company go up. I saw it and felt it until my heart expanded with tears of gratitude, then completely let go. Immediately upon coming out of meditation, I saw that my stock value had tripled since the morning due to an unexpected announcement from the CEO. Another time, I wanted to know what it would feel like to have a partner who reflected all of what was in my heart. I sat in that feeling in meditation for the better part of an hour because of the joy I had in the feeling. Later that day, at 1:14 pm Pacific Time to be precise, I saw that I had received a text sent at exactly 1:14 Mountain Time from an unknown number. 1:14 is a special number for me, like a wink from God, because my birthday is January 14. It turned out to be an old friend who felt inspired to reach out to me right at that moment, an old friend who a short time later turned out to be the manifestation of that emotion.

Perhaps my favorite manifestation is actually Jenn's. She decided she wanted a vine garden with watermelons and other fruits in the place of our giant rock bed out back. She envisioned it, felt it, and then came and asked me to do the work (her idea of manifestation at the time). I told her I wanted no part of it. The rocks had to be pulled out, the weed cloth removed, dirt put in, and finally the seeds planted. Although she meant to go ahead and do the work on her own, she forgot about it. In about a month, there were vines growing all over the rock bed anyway. No rocks had been moved, the weed cloth was still there, no dirt had been added, and importantly, no seeds had been planted. Nothing grew in that spot the year before. Now, there were watermelons, cantaloupes, pumpkins, and some kind of native Texas gourd growing in every direction. We had more watermelon than we could eat with a family of nine.

The types of experiences we can manifest are without limit. To the degree that they are limited, it is because our minds have not yet expanded to the point that we can authentically *feel* the emotion and let go of attachment to the outcome. Sometimes it is best to start with manifestations that stretch the imagination, but only slightly. It is easier to manifest that which the mind does not resist and/or does not care about. Such as the story I told in my previous book, *Faith to Produce Miracles.* I was coming home with my oldest daughter after lunch saying what a perfect day it had been. I then said, "The only thing that would make this day more perfect are some brownies!" We both laughed, but when we arrived home, there was a pan of brownies on the door step.

A week later, she and I were walking together and she said, "Dad, do you remember how last week we manifest those brownies? I want to do that again, only this time, I want mint chocolate chip brownies!" We laughed again at the ridiculousness of how insignificant such a request must seem to God – as if that would ever happen!

So, I added with equal playfulness, "See that property over there with the creek running through it? I want to meditate there whenever I want." It was a beautiful piece of private property up against the Tetons that we definitely could not afford at the time. An hour later, however, some of our new neighbors came to introduce themselves carrying a pan of brownies with some kind of a green frosting on top. Caroline and I both perked up instantly.

"What are those?" I asked probingly.

"Mint chocolate chip brownies," our new neighbors responded. Later in the conversation, we also discovered they were the owners of most of the property in the area, including the place with the creek where I wanted to meditate. They gave me permission to go there anytime I wanted.

All of those manifestations would come much later, however. In that moment with Father, I was still fascinated with the mechanism of the Light itself and how it expanded heaven. It would take me several years to understand how the same principle in heaven is functional on earth, and that we could use it to alter our present state of being in this life. It was simply a matter of connecting what Jesus had shown me about the transition of the earth with what God was showing me about our ability to create in the Light.

It took me several years to really learn how to manifest well, but even shortly after this experience, I began to experiment with manifestation far more frequently. In fact, I did not truly realize how much popular teachings of manifestation overlapped with my experience until I saw Dr. Joe Dispenza at the Santa Fe Advanced Seminar in February of 2018. He went into a discussion of the physics of manifestation and I thought, *For the first time I have heard someone put the physics of what I experienced into English!*

After Father finished teaching me about the Light and how it worked, I departed from His presence. I do not remember how or why, but I was taken and shown a friend who was tearfully pleading with God in the temple. I understood her to be one of those lights on the earth that Jesus had shown me I would interact with. I could see she was struggling with questions that resembled ones that had been in my own heart. I was given the answer she was seeking and was instructed to share it with her, similar to how we might think of a guardian angel doing. I could see her, but she did not appear to have any awareness of my presence. However, she seemed to feel the words I communicated, like a warm blanket of understanding, which she perceived as a direct answer from God. My role as a messenger in this case was completely transparent, allowing her direct communion with God as though there were no messenger.

I remember the joy at being able to serve her in that way. It seemed to be an honor. A few days later, after I had returned from my experience, I spoke to her. I was able to confirm that this friend had indeed been at the temple praying when I saw her, and that she had received the answer I was instructed to share with her through the veil. This caused me to wonder how many times I had received inspiration, understanding, or comfort from unseen angelic visitors. It also led me to ponder whether there was really much difference between heavenly angels and those who are still are on the earth. At least in this instance, I had been able to participate in a heavenly experience for someone even while my body was still alive. In many near-death experiences, those who had the experience find some degree of validation when they realize that a conversation or event they saw others having while out of their body was verifiable in real life. The same was true for me in this experience with my friend in the temple.

As my experience on the other side came to an end, I do not recall any formal goodbyes. I was simply left to drift in the light. It was like waking up from a deep sleep – only as I did so, I found that I was still in that spiritual state of feeling infinite bliss while being connected to my body. It was like I had never left Father's presence.

Chapter 7

Reintegrating into the World

While the first experience of crossing over changed me in subtle, almost unnoticeable ways, this second experience completely changed my demeanor and the way that I showed up in the world around me. While mere seconds in that space can communicate untold volumes, this time I was there for several hours. I was certain that I had seen God in the same way as people who have had near-death experiences. I had a peace I had never known in all of my life and it was tangible to those around me even several weeks after my experience. I knew things about people and events without being told.

For starters, I immediately interacted with Jenn and our children. She had seen me when the experience started, so it was only natural to share with her. I did not think twice about it, and my body was still on fire with uncontrollable tears when I returned. I could not have hid what I was experiencing from them if I had tried. Nor did it occur to me to do so.

However, I was also still thinking and feeling in a spiritual state where words are not necessary to communicate. It was as though my body was moving but my spirit had not fully returned. I simply willed my family to understand as though the spiritual communication was all that was needed. So, while they could see the intensity of what I was feeling internally, I do not know how much sense my words made to them at the time.

I did feel to specifically bless my children, where I saw and spoke beautiful words about their future. Afterward, I asked what they were feeling and noticing. A couple of them said they felt or could see angels present. My son said that he could hear them speaking to him.

I have heard many sad stories of how those who have seen something so beautiful on the other side were unable to speak with anyone of their experience for most of their lives. That which was so sacred to them was ridiculed even by those closest to them anytime they tried to share it. I was fortunate that my wife and children were very receptive to all that I had to say and share. Jenn seemed to see this side of me even before these events happened, like she was just waiting for it to sprout, and did all she could to support me.

While the children in their innocence simply accepted all that I said, Jenn and I talked often about the nature of what I had experienced and what it meant for our family. The nature of what she felt in my words caused her to change her own relationship with God. She was starting to feel more of her worth before God and to believe that she could have these experiences too. The questions she was asking were awakening her own understanding even as mine began to open.

Outside of my immediate family, I did not share this experience with many others. There were one or two exceptions of individuals who had previously shared their own experience of seeing Jesus with me. I felt like the leap of faith they took with me had created a safe space for me to reciprocate. It felt beautiful to share with them, but too sacred to speak to anyone else. It was not the right time, and the freshness of it still had my mouth shut with unspeakable joy.

For that matter, I had very little desire to interact with anyone else that I used to interact with. It was clear to me that my life had changed and that I was no longer to participate in many of the groups I had been part of before. Specifically, I had little to no desire to participate in the meetings that discussed apocalyptic events. Nothing in my experience touched upon the prophesied destruction, and besides, what I had seen leading up to the earth's transition was beautiful! Also, God had shown me the manner in which we co-create all that is. I knew that what we focus on is created.

The violent destruction of the world foretold in Biblical scripture was not meant to happen anymore than Jonah's prophecy of the destruction of Nineveh. After finally delivering his prophecy, he went up on a hill to watch the fireworks begin. After much time passed, he grew angry with God that Nineveh had not yet been destroyed.[15] Like many of us today, he did not understand that what had been written was not written so that it would happen, but so that the people might choose a new future. As Jesus said to James and John when they wanted to call fire down on the people who rejected him, "Ye know not what manner of spirit ye are of. For the Son of man is not come to destroy men's lives, but to save them."[16]

It is true that the world must change, but how it changes is up to us. I had seen that to the degree that a small amount of leavening was awakened in the global consciousness, the events of the transition of the earth could be significantly altered if not entirely bypassed. We could choose to ascend in joy if that were the desire of our hearts. Therefore, my obsession with apocalyptic scripture completely disappeared as I realized that what we put in our hearts contributes to how that transition unfolds. I determined to use my faith only to create a more positive transition for the earth.

But it wasn't just my relationship with the various groups in Utah discussing the events leading up to the Second Coming that changed. Even my internal state of being relative to church was completely changed in accordance with how my beliefs and understanding were altered in the experience. Church for the entirety of my adult life had been a given, a necessary part of life that was never questioned. It just was. I felt greater dependence upon it for my role and value in life than oxygen. Yet, now that emotion of need was gone. And I don't mean just a little gone; it was completely gone.

I felt whole and completely enveloped by God for the first time in my life. Returning to a belief that I was separate from Him by participating in various religious activities seemed to deny the experience of deep and abiding connection I felt. I soon realized the cocoon is for the caterpillar, not the butterfly. God had made

---

[15] Jonah 4:1-11

[16] Luke 9:55-56

me free. Also, I no longer felt that I could freely share what I was experiencing in a church setting. For one, I did not yet have the vocabulary to communicate what I had seen; even if I did, what place does the experience of the butterfly have among those who are still experiencing the transformation in the cocoon?

And yet, unlike some who become bitter with the religions of this world, I had no desire to interfere with the religion of my young adulthood. While the butterfly that has not yet emerged from its cocoon may fight to be free from what feels like a suffocating prison, the fully emerged butterfly is able to see the beauty in the loving womb that formed it. The butterfly does not resent the cocoon. In fact, as with child birth, resistance just slows the process down and makes it more painful. The miracle to take place is facilitated with surrender. In my case, I could see that the rigidity of the cocoon of religious structure that I had chosen was matched to the kind of butterfly I was to become. Even though my own needs had changed, I could still see the beauty in what religion was contributing to our overall human experience. I also knew that I did not have all the answers as to the purpose of religion in this world, and I was willing to hold space for the deeper understanding I knew would someday emerge.

My experience also contributed to my patience with not having those answers just yet. The experience on the other side was of having all knowledge present, but not necessarily being consciously aware of it. There was no feeling of lack or fear in this regard, because as soon as a question materialized, the answer had already been given in full with all of its tangents. This resulted in a loss of urgency to know the answer because all answers were just a thought away. It was safe to be held in absolute love without needing to know. This is similar to how schools have deemphasized the need to memorize facts now that anything can be found with a quick internet search. When you know all the answers are just a fingertip away, you can relax. I did not need to understand all things in this moment, because God did. And that was enough.

Since I returned with a memory of what it was like to be comfortable even without all the answers, I did not feel a need to demand answers for the contradictions between what I experienced and what religions sometimes teach. Therefore, I neither resisted nor needed an ongoing church experience. With very little to offer or gain from church at that time, my attendance was reduced to merely a means of staying connected with my family and friends who still found it important. I knew God loved me. There was no question. I could feel it in every moment. In fact, the spiritual intensity of that state, almost to the degree that I had during the experience itself, lasted for several weeks. The peace was tangible to those I met during that time. I even entertained the thought that those feelings would never go away.

One of the ideas that was communicated to me without words during my experience was that I had a standing invitation to return to that place and state of being as often as I desired. In fact, I was not only invited, I was expected to return. I was to come back as often as possible, going deeper and deeper. For even with all that I had experienced, I had only experienced a drop in an infinite ocean of love and bliss. I had not arrived at an end-point. Rather, I was merely beginning a journey. This led to a dramatic change in the amount of time I spent in prayer and meditation and the way that I experienced them. Rather than just an hour a day, I would spend the greater part of each day in prayer and meditation. Since I was still provided for financially, this replaced my job as it were.

I saw the connection between the invitation to go deeper and the rising of the earth. Each time we use prayer, meditation, or other spiritual activities to start breaking down the veil between us and God, the amount of light we experience increases. When we come back from that experience, a portion of that light remains with us. We get brighter and brighter individually, and thus collectively.

As we use this process to purify matter by releasing the subconscious beliefs within consciousness at a personal level, it affects the consciousness present in the light in all sentient beings. Like a pebble thrown into a still pond causing ripples, so too does our release of patterns within the veil of humanity cause a ripple effect throughout all creation. As more of us start penetrating the veil in even small degrees, a greater amount of light becomes available not only for us individually, but for humanity collectively. Therefore, one of the greatest acts of love we can give in this life is to go so deeply into the bosom of the divine that all we know is forever changed. It is to let God love us with a love that we have not earned and that God never intended or wanted us to earn, because it was always grace. The release in us also liberates the world around us.

All of this contributed to our family decision to move to the Tetons in Wyoming. We no longer felt connected to any location or idea, so I asked each of the kids separately to close their eyes and envision a location on the map where we would have the most joy. Every single one of them, including the ones who were feeling a little peevish, saw the same location – a place we had never been to before. Jenn and I simply exchanged glances. The camper was already packed. We were ready to start our next adventure.

Part 3

Heaven is Bigger

Chapter 8

Tools to Raise the Earth

As I had more experiences with the other side, my view of the world increasingly changed. I no longer saw the world as entirely separate from me. That is, I no longer saw events in the world as strictly happening to me as though I were a victim. Rather, I saw them increasingly arising in synchronicity with the beliefs that were in my heart and the hearts of others in this world. Jesus had shown me the programs that exist within consciousness that give rise to the way we experience life – specifically the separation we perceive from God. He had shown me that those programs were not fixed in a permanent way by the decree of an external God. Rather, we were unconsciously creating them and to the degree that we woke up to their nature, we had the power to change reality for ourselves and the whole of the world around us. He was literally waiting on us to wake up, waiting on us to discover the deeper meaning of unquenchable love hidden behind the cultural understanding of judgment in the world's religions. We were co-creating that transition with God. This was the meaning of the faith that was to precede the return of Christ consciousness in the world.

However, as I pondered these truths within my heart, I became aware of the limitations of the tools I had been given up to that point. While I had felt God's love on numerous occasions in church settings, my entire relationship with Jesus and God revolved around an external understanding. My spiritual practice was focused on external obedience, including control of my actions, thoughts, and/or emotions with an eye toward improving my state in the hereafter. Nowhere in my upbringing was there any understanding of the underlying programs creating the veil that Jesus had shown me, nor of the means to access and change them in order to release that veil in this life. There were few to no references to these ideas in my religion or even in Christian scripture.

However, the experience I had with Jesus made it clear to me that the understandings necessary to access these programs were already present somewhere on the earth. Just because they were absent from my cultural understanding didn't mean that the knowledge was not already present elsewhere. In fact, I could distinctly remember the lights He showed me across the face of the earth representing people who were coming through the veil into His presence. When I saw them, I understood these were not all from the same culture – I knew from my interaction with Him that God's work and his love were much bigger than that. He was speaking to all of his children, each in their own language and understanding. Each were being given truths to lift the whole, and it was only through overcoming our fears and prejudices that we would be able to assemble the puzzle of unlocking the love of God on earth. I just needed to let go of the boundaries I had in place of how and where God could teach me.

I felt hope swell up inside me that my experience with Jesus and with Father could continue to progress as I learned to access those programs and release them. I no longer saw my relationship with Jesus through the limitations I had been given in my cultural understanding. I now saw those teachings as the stepping stone preparing me for real experience in the presence of God. In light of my own experiences, my understanding had become a living entity no longer dependent on anyone else's opinion or interpretation of scripture. In fact, my definition of scripture was changing just as quickly, from only those words found in the Bible uttered by God's prophets, to all that the Light revealed in every moment. I saw that there was a hidden language, as it were, behind every thought, emotion, and experience in life. Each moment was filled with the light of God in which the light was our teacher. The truth was broadcasting in every moment where life itself became the word of God, revealing the way as it has always existed, both in our hearts and in the heart of God. This light could reveal to our understandings what words never could.

This understanding and awareness gave me courage to step beyond the bounds of my past limitations. Even those I previously thought of as being "deceived," I now saw in a new context. They may have been on a different path from my own, but it did not make them any less sincere in their approach to find God or make meaning from life. Just like when I was at the university, my path may have been bioengineering, but that didn't mean I couldn't learn from those who were business teachers or legal teachers. In fact, it was only by virtue of taking the understanding that each of those other disciplines offered that I was able to be so successful in developing science that would truly impact the world.

In a similar way, those on various spiritual paths taught the understanding they had found to be true in their own lives. It remained for me to mine the light from the teachings in those disparate paths in order to truly understand what Jesus was trying to show me and lay out before me. I wanted access to all truth, not just that truth which was found in my culture. The only question I needed to answer was – where are the teachings that will help me access the programs that create the veil? So, I asked God to direct me to those tools, excited for the new adventure I sensed was in front of me.

As had happened on numerous occasions before, in response to the question, the answers came. I was invited to a group meeting in Utah with individuals discussing spiritual gifts present in other cultures. One woman was there who had recently been initiated into Reiki. Reiki, which is Japanese for the "life force energy" (ki) of "God's wisdom" (Rei), is a healing technique where a practitioner channels light to help an individual open to inner healing.

The woman, whose name I do not remember, told us about her own prayers and being led to practice Reiki. For her, it was one of the ways God allowed His light to enter the world. She said that after receiving her attunements (the formal initiation into Reiki), she began to see angels and others from the other side. She broke into tears that I felt in the center of my being as she described how her connection with Jesus had increased dramatically since that time. She also tearfully talked about her conversations with her religious leaders surrounding her newfound sensitivity to God's love. As she was part of a conservative Christian religion, she had been fearful of how they would respond. However, they reacted differently than she expected, encouraging her to follow what was being put in her heart.

This impacted me profoundly. I saw in her story a potential answer to my own prayers. I wanted to see more, so I asked her to show me what she was talking about. She proceeded to do a Reiki session with me and helped me find one of the blocks that had been preventing me from feeling more of God's love. I was astounded at how quickly this tool helped me to find areas of unresolved hurt within my heart and to create deep, healing changes. While I was still uncertain about Reiki or similar traditions, I knew that what I experienced was exactly what I had been praying to find – a tool to help me more quickly find and heal the programs keeping me separate from the moment-to-moment experience of the love of God. I knew without more advanced ways of interacting with God, I would never be able to truly wake up to that heavenly joy in this life.

The spiritual healing I received also reminded me of a story in the Bible. I remembered the words of the blindman healed by Jesus when the Pharisees accused Jesus of being a sinner for not following their rules, "Why herein is a marvelous thing, that ye know not from whence he is, and yet he hath opened mine eyes. Now we know that God heareth not sinners: but if any man be a worshipper of God, and doeth his will, him he heareth... If this man were not of God, he could do nothing." [17] I had been healed of a deep wound in my relationship with God opening me to feel more of His love and in direct answer to my prayer. My "eyes" had been opened spiritually. I understood from the scripture that just like Jesus with the blind man, there was no way this woman could have answered my prayers if her actions were not inspired by God.

---

[17] John 9:30-33

I promptly went home and prayed, "God, is this what you were trying to show me? Is this part of what I'm supposed to learn?" I immediately felt that expanse of light in the center of my being that told me I was on the right track, followed by a voice in my heart and mind, "Not only are the lessons from energy healing part of what you should learn, it is central to it."

After talking with Jenn about what I was feeling, I asked various friends who I knew had explored other paths to share with me their experiences. I didn't know enough to really understand what they were saying, or how to evaluate the different paths. I just had faith that when they mentioned something connected to my future path, I would feel the light in my heart expand. My internal compass would tell me where to go.

"What was that last thing you said?" I asked Julie. I wasn't certain what she had just said to me, but my heart suddenly lit up like a light bulb.

"Matrix Energetics," she answered. "It's an energy healing modality."

I had no idea what Matrix Energetics was and still only had a vague concept of what energy healing was. However, in answer to my prayer about where I could go to find greater understanding, I felt the expanse in my heart about Matrix Energetics. Years of trusting that feeling plus the excitement over the potential to learn tools to experience in the flesh what Jesus had shown me in vision caused me to move beyond the boundaries of past comfort zones.

Chapter 9

Consciousness and the Quantum World

There was a Matrix Energetics conference being held in Albuquerque, New Mexico just a few weeks later. The whole family decided to make a trip of it and we drove to New Mexico together. Richard Bartlett, the founder of Matrix Energetics, was on stage that night with Melissa Joy Jonsson. I didn't know it at the time, but I couldn't have been led to a better conference considering my background.

That first night at the conference, I watched person after person get up on stage. They would appear to swoon and then their physiology frequently changed right before our eyes. While watching intently, my older son, James, caught my attention, "Dad, look at David!" David is my third child and had always taken an interest in church and spiritual matters. At that very moment, David was swaying around in a circle with a dazed expression on his face.

"Dad, look!" James repeated. "I can poke him and he doesn't do anything!"

Of course, my older son's interest would be in the fact that he could torment his brother without response. But this had me curious. What was David doing?

"Stop poking your brother," I reprimanded James. Before I could get any further, David suddenly fell out of his chair onto the floor.

"David, David!" I exclaimed as I rushed over to check on him. "Are you ok?"

David looked at me with bleary eyes. "Dad," he said slowly. "I need to come to this conference."

A little surprised, I asked, "What do you mean?"

"I need to come," he responded still in a daze. "God wants me to be here."

I didn't know how to respond to that. The idea of energy healing was new to me and the conference wasn't cheap. We were still at the free introduction, but the full conference cost around a thousand dollars for the weekend and children often have fickle minds. However, I had never seen him act this way before. I came to a decision.

"David, how about I go to this one. I'll share with you what I learn when I get back. If you still feel you need to go after that, I'll take you to the next one."

David's experience was enough for me to validate my own impressions to be at this conference. David was not a hand-picked volunteer. He couldn't have been planted in the audience. He was my son. And he had just fallen to the floor in a swoon and received personal direction from God matching my own about attending this conference.

The next day, I absorbed the explanations both Richard and Melissa gave for what we were witnessing. They explained that the experience of our world is not all it appears to be. Consciousness dwells in the center of patterns of information that we use to both interpret and create experience. To the extent that we remain locked into the reasons our mind gives us for why our world is the way it is, our physical world is solid and unchangeable. The weaknesses we were born with are bound to stick to us forever. However, the more we realize the story is illusion, the more permission we give ourselves for change. Our world is only unchangeable because the rigidity in our hearts makes it so. We can return to a state of consciousness prior to our interpretation of what it should be like and create a new experience. This change in the program of consciousness has the potential to bring about instantaneous shift in the hologram of life.

Only Richard and Melissa didn't use exactly those words. Rather, Richard said, "The universe is a Boston Terrier, and you've got the ball." Knowing some of us needed a more logical explanation to Richard's colorful remarks, Melissa made a reference to quantum physics, "You're accessing the space before the collapse of the wave-function and then choosing a new possibility from the space of infinite potential."

Quantum physics describes the properties of extremely small molecules that make up atoms. These molecules do not behave the way we expect our world to behave. For example, if you throw a basketball at a wall you expect it to bounce off every time. There is no way it will disappear and reappear on the other side. However, the same is not true for quantum particles. One of their hallmark characteristics is that they exist as both matter and energy. It would not be out of the ordinary at all for a quantum molecule to disappear and reappear on the other side of a barrier. In fact, many scientific technologies are built on this principle.

Even more bizarre is the fact that quantum physicists have proven that human consciousness actually affects the probability a quantum particle will disappear and reappear on the other side of the "wall." This effect holds true even when the people trying to affect the particles' behavior are on the other side of the world or are trying to influence a particle's behavior at another time point (i.e. before or even after the experiment has been run).

While using conscious thought to affect a quantum particle smaller than an atom may not excite many people, those who can put two and two together realize that we are made entirely of quantum particles and so is the world around us. Therefore, if these particles change with conscious observation, then what does that mean about our bodies and the world around us when we change the deep thoughts of our hearts?

There are plenty of people quick to point out that this might be the mechanism of how faith interacts with our physical world. For that matter, quantum scientists are in absolute agreement that consciousness does affect the individual quantum particles that make up our world. However, what they are still uncertain of is why that happens or what that means for the real world around us. The scientific data has not yet been able to show causation of macro-events in the world from the provable connection between conscious thought and quantum behavior.

In that moment, however, I didn't need a body of scientific literature. I was witnessing spinal curvature disappear in the blink of any eye. Physical maladies were in many cases being spontaneously healed. From my perspective, it appeared Richard truly was capitalizing on the ability to shift his consciousness into a space where the full potential of the quantum particle existed. Reality could be anything. It just needed space within the bounds of our heart for new opportunities to emerge.

We were told the healing effects were not dependent on what each of us had learned in our religious or spiritual backgrounds. In fact, Richard also told us that the healing happened best to the extent we let go of what we thought we knew. The moment we stop trying to limit God by putting Him in the box of our understanding, we allow Him to be what He is, and give Him permission to do amazing things. In other words, the Intelligence that makes up the world around us was willing to respond to us – all we needed to do was to trust enough to let go of our understanding, metaphorically throwing the ball for the Boston Terrier to chase.

That seemed too simple to be true, but we were already being sent off for our first experiences. As we broke out into groups to apply what we had learned, I was partnered with a woman who was also there for the first time. Not knowing what I was doing, I simply went through the motions.

In less time than either of us knew what was happening, she landed with a crash on her backside on the floor, causing both of us to start laughing hysterically.

"What happened?" I asked through fits of laughter.

"I don't know. I just fell down," she said still laughing. "Oh my God! I can hear out of my ear again!"

"Seriously? You mean you couldn't hear before?"

"Just out of the one ear," she answered. "I lost hearing out of it around seven years ago."

By now, there was a small group around us equally curious about what was happening. "Oh wait!" she exclaimed. "I can taste salt water. How weird is that?"

"Salt water – why salt water?" I asked, now thoroughly confused.

"Oh my God! Oh my God! Oh my God!" she exclaimed with a look like she had just received a huge insight. "I was at the beach when I first lost my hearing. There was this huge wave and it knocked my head into the sand. I bet that's what the salt water is from!"

There was a tangible feeling of sacred respect in the small group around us now. Only, it was also filled with the laughter of little children who have just discovered joy in something completely unexpected.

But this was only the start of my adventures that weekend. I was moved into spiritual states of consciousness I did not know existed. Each time, those on the other side who had been speaking to me in times of prayer for years took the opportunity to speak to me without the usual walls I had in place. It was like the static that had been interfering with the signal on the heavenly radio was suddenly gone. Long-standing patterns and beliefs systems opened, creating space that had not been present within me before.

With all of these new experiences, I hungrily interviewed every person I met at the conference, curious about their backgrounds. Like me, each felt spiritually called to be there. Although we had different understandings of who or what God was, each of us felt called by the Divine to attend. This caused me to reflect on my own instruction. Was the way I had been led by Jesus better than the way they had been led? Or had each of these different paths somehow brought us all to the same place and the same time to the same conclusion?

I pondered deeply about the meaning of this. We were each from different spiritual backgrounds and belief systems. Was it possible that our separate journeys, despite the huge differences in our former understanding, could lead us to similar insights?

What was I truly supposed to be learning? Was it healing, or was it something even more important about our individual journeys to God?

I came back to conference after conference. At each one, my body kept changing, physically, emotionally and mentally. A back injury that I had been dealing with for roughly ten years suddenly disappeared. Previously, I had been in chronic pain and had acute bouts with my spine slipping out of position leaving me literally paralyzed on the floor at times. Years of physical therapy, chiropractors, medical prescriptions, and massage therapists had not touched it. And yet one day on the plane ride back from one of the seminars, I was playing with what I had learned and the pain simply disappeared. There was no trace of it. It was just gone as though it had never existed. There were no shining lights, heavenly visions, or powerful flows of energy. Nothing. It was just gone. My mind was reeling from what I was experiencing.

I reflected that this was definitely the type of tool set I had prayed to find. Our progression back to God did not need to be limited to what our conscious mind could learn or understand. I was experiencing a nonlinear form of learning where my understanding could make the same types of leaps as a quantum particle. I knew that if this world was to ever become like the visions I had of heaven, then we would need to experience awakening at a level that exceeded the highest rates at which our conscious minds could learn. We needed quantum shifts in both individual and global consciousness. While I understood that Matrix Energetics was only a beginning relative to the types of healing and learning I believed would exist in the future, I felt it pointed me toward an understanding of a higher form and definition of faith.

I could see clearly now that faith is not what is most commonly taught in world religions. It is not something that comes from clinging to an idea – no matter how beautiful or worthy we may think it is. It is not a form of mental constipation where we squeeze and push with our minds to try to obtain an outcome. It isn't desperately clinging to what we believe is true or what we may have been told even in vision. Nor is it purifying the one little part of the mind we are aware of by suppressing undesirable thoughts and emotions. It isn't about earning a blessing through our perceived "righteousness" or the size of our commitment to God as exhibited through personal sacrifice. It isn't a ritual of religious practice or even the level of desperation behind our beggings and pleadings with the Divine. All of these things are actually more like expressions of doubt. Real faith that produces powerful change is almost the opposite. It is about letting go. It is surrender. It is an expansion of the heart that we experience when we stop fighting and open to new possibility. The change available in that moment of release is far more than the sum total of all our other efforts combined.

Chapter 10

Twelve Paths to Zion and Cookie-Dough Ice Cream

Back home in Utah, thoughts about my experiences with those of other spiritual backgrounds continued to tug at my soul. These thoughts were amplified because of the number of groups in Utah I met with who claimed to be interested in helping the earth transition into a higher state. However, unlike the harmony among those of different religious backgrounds I saw at the Matrix Energetics conferences, these groups tended to have the same rigid mindset I observed in the more mainstream religious communities: "There is only path to God, and it is mine."

The irony in the discord between these groups was that each was talking about building Zion, the city of one heart and mind! Not all the groups I encountered used the word "Zion," because not all came from the same religious background or understanding. But each described the same principle. No matter which group I met with, each talked about the coming transition of the world into a higher state. Each talked about communities living a higher law in a higher consciousness where there was no more pain or fear. So, how could they view others who were equally sincere as being misled or outright deceived?

In hindsight, I guess part of the problem was that they were each having very real experiences with God and their experiences appeared to contradict each other. In their worldview, they had the answer to the whole puzzle, not just a piece of it. Since each knew the veracity of their own experience, the only thing they could doubt was the other person or group. Since, their own experience was "true," the experiences of everyone else must be "false," or at least grossly misunderstood.

This highly paradoxical situation was a lot like the parable of the six blindmen and the elephant. In the parable, six blindmen, never having seen or heard of an elephant before, each encounter the animal for the first time. One finds the trunk and describes the elephant as a large, writhing snake. Another touches the tusks and vehemently argues that the elephant is not like a snake at all, but like a spear. Still a third encounters the side of the elephant and protests that the other two are deceived: an elephant is like a wall.

This comedic encounter goes on with the others finding the ear, the tail, and the leg of the elephant respectively. The argument is all the more heated, not because of the incorrect experience of each of the blindmen, but because of their *very real* experience. It was the truth they had already experienced that blinded them all the more to receiving more truth; being blind, they could not comprehend how more than one truth about the elephant could simultaneously apply.

Likewise, among all these circles of friends who I knew had sacred encounters with God, each was only seeing part of the elephant. Because we are blind to what we don't know yet, we tend to defend what we feel is true rather than to sincerely listen to the experience of others.

It was in this state of mind that I met with a friend one night at Cold Stone after a group meeting. Commenting on the differences between the groups, I said, "I just don't understand how two people who've seen God can be so antagonistic toward each other. It's almost like they have different paths to Zion."

"Ok. So… what do you mean?" my friend prompted. This was a regular give and take for us to bring out new thoughts and observations.

"I mean, what if there isn't just one approach to Zion?" I questioned. "What if each of these groups represents a different approach, and it's the truths in their own approach that causes them to feel like the others are misled?"

I continued to digest this thought while looking for the last pieces of cookie dough floating around in my quickly melting ice cream.

"Wait!" I exclaimed. "Revelation says there are twelve gates into the New Jerusalem, one for each of the twelve tribes of

Israel.[18] Isn't gate just another word for a path of entry? So, Revelation could be telling us there are twelve different ways or paths to enter the state of one heart and mind!"

I was getting excited now. Previously, I had not been able to reconcile the differences among my various groups of friends. But what if their differences weren't a problem? What if we were supposed to have differences? Maybe those differences were an important part of the rising of the earth. If so, then the loyalty each group felt to their own perspective was justified. They were simply focused on the gate they had been called to enter.

As frequently happens when we open to a new understanding, confirmation of this idea started to surface fairly quickly. Another friend gave me a book series, *The Immortal*, about John the Revelator. I wasn't that interested in the storyline, so I just flipped open to a random page in the second book. It just happened to be the passage where the author describes being taken up in a vision with John the Revelator into the heavenly city of one heart and one mind. He sees the twelve gates leading into the city and notes that no one can enter except through their appointed gate. He then asks an amazingly insightful question:

I have always assumed the ultimate goal for humans was oneness and unity of some kind. So my question is: Why are there twelve entrances into the city? Why was I only permitted to go through one of them?[19]

John's answer is no less insightful, speaking directly to my own thoughts:

The purpose of the twelve entrances is the oneness that you mentioned... The twelve different entrances represent, for

---

[18] Revelation 21:12

[19] Dewey, JJ. (1998) *The Immortal, Book Two*. [Kindle Version]

want of a better word, twelve different thought patterns that humanity gravitates toward. Each person of pure intent can be fairly united within his own pattern, but has great difficulty in harmonizing with another outside his pattern. That is part of the reason a good Jew, for instance, can see eye-to-eye with another Jew of similar thought, but may feel the Hindu or Christian is misled. His thought patterns will not let him see the beauty of other religions, patterns or philosophies." John continues to explain that once a person enters the city through demonstrating unity with their own thought pattern, they then go on to achieve unity with the truth in all of the other thought patterns until they comprehend a fullness of the light in God.

I could not believe what I was reading. Had I not just had this discussion at Cold Stone? Was this not exactly what I was proposing? Had I not asked God for confirmation if this idea was real? The fictional context of the book was beside the point – I found truth in those words.

As I pondered the significance of what I had just read, I remembered a related passage from *Visions of Glory*. I immediately ran and grabbed the book and flipped it open to the author's description of Zion. In it, he too saw that Zion had twelve gates. Each one was for a different people who brought their own religious leaders and scriptures. Each had their own temple where they received the spiritual understandings and rites of passage of their people. There was also a temple in the center of the city where, presumably, unity amongst the different schools of thought was taught.[20] Previously, I had assumed that each of those religious leaders and scriptures would conform to my own. But what if this referred to multiple paths to the same collective god-consciousness?

With these two seeming confirmations, my excitement only continued to grow. But as much as I thought I had received a

---

[20] Pontius, J. (2012) *Visions of Glory*. Springville, UT: Cedar Fort, Inc, pg 186

confirmation of this concept through the spontaneous appearance of the writings of others, I was yet to receive a much more direct understanding just a couple weeks later.

Chapter 11

Third Experience: Seeing God through the Eyes of Another

By this point I had seen and heard enough in my various experiences that my traditional ways of thinking had begun to loosen. Jesus was leading me to receive initiations in paths outside of my own. Matrix Energetics was among the first of those, which encouraged me to seek for others. I sent out the heart-felt manifestation that the teachers I was looking for to initiate me into these different paths would find me. However, rather than spending another twenty years in a different religion or philosophy, I wanted to find teachers who understood the deepest truths of these paths who were willing to depart from tradition and initiate me into those understandings in an afternoon.

While I was open to which paths God might use to teach me, one of the paths I wanted to be initiated into was Reiki. The memory of the woman who told me about her experiences with God during her Reiki attunements was still with me. What was more, many of my friends shared similar stories of experiences during their attunements. I felt in my heart, that if I received my attunements, I would have another experience of heaven. However, I had little interest in Reiki outside of the experience I knew was waiting for me. I did not want to take the classes or pay for attunements. I wanted to manifest someone showing up and telling me that they were inspired to give them to me. And then, rather than giving them to me over a number of weeks or months according to Reiki custom, I wanted to receive them all in an afternoon.

And so it happened that I met a woman who was a Reiki master. As we talked, it turned out she had experiences with Jesus similar to my own. This led to a beautiful conversation where we each shared the sacred events in our hearts that we so rarely had the opportunity to tell. After opening our hearts in this way, she confided in me that she felt guided to give me all four attunements and that she was supposed to depart from tradition to give them to me in a single session.

I was definitely excited. Up to that point, I still hadn't told her of my desire. Yet, this was my manifestation come to pass in very deed. And because it was so recognizable, I felt it was a confirmation that the heavens were about to open in an unprecedented way for me.

As she began the process of giving the attunements, I immediately felt sacred energy all around me and through me. It no longer felt like the woman I had been talking to, but my Heavenly Mother. The feeling entered me with such suddenness that it was like I was in a whole different place. That love was more than anything I had ever known. I lost all emotional control and began to weep openly. My heart was still so open from my previous crossover experiences, that I do not know that my being fully separated from my body. I could just see and feel everything as though I were already in another place outside of time. I was no longer Brent who was receiving an attunement on earth, but a being who existed before and who will exist after, standing in the presence of God, receiving sacred rituals and ceremonies which had nothing to do with what was taking place below. I could feel it with intensity throughout my being.

If the feeling of Mother ministering to me had been all, I would have been happy. But what followed next broke what few understandings of the structure of heaven I thought I had left. I was about to have a whole series of memories return to me in greater clarity than any memory I have of this life. In fact, I was to see some of the most sacred events from other lifetimes that left me trembling all over. Whether these memories were actually "mine" or were provided as-though-they-were-mine does not matter to me. They were more real than the majority of experiences I have had in this life and I have learned from them in profound and sacred ways.

I do not remember exactly how I moved into the first memory, but it seemed to me almost like there was a nodal point in the light that came into my heart. This nodal point was like an intersection of multiple lifetimes. Only, it was not abstract the way we might think of a nodal point. It was more like a living intelligence, a higher version of myself that was more aware of the branches of life that had been taken.

No sooner did the light enter into me than I found myself seeing through the eyes of another person in a city somewhere in mainland China. The people around me were speaking Mandarin and I was speaking it in return to them. Buildings were stacked on top of each other with numerous signs in Mandarin hanging from the sides of the buildings. In later years, I looked at pictures of China to try to identify the time period. The architecture and signs in larger Chinese cities from the mid 1800's to early 1900's best match what I saw. Somehow, I was experiencing the sensations and emotions of this individual as seen through his eyes while simultaneously feeling the reactions of my present self to those experiences. It was like being both and more, almost like I was the awareness in both individuals and yet also the one observing them. I did not perceive him as separate from me. It was the same way we experience our memories and our day-to-day life. That is, that sense of knowing that says, "This is me, and this is my experience." There was no question of it, I just knew this was me.

The memories were not random events. Rather, they focused on a single spiritual event that was likely the culmination of that lifetime. I saw that I was part of an eastern religion similar to Buddhism. I had devoted my entire life in that discipline even as I had devoted this life to Christ. But what astounded me is that I experienced coming into the presence of my since-departed Master in that life and the feeling was exactly the same as when I came into the presence of Jesus in this life.

Through the eyes of Lao Tzen, as I was called, I saw my Master in spiritual form and experienced that same explosion of love, joy, and even salvation beyond measure. I wept and wept and wept. It was indeed the same feeling as my present-self had in coming into the presence of Christ. It was that same feeling of intense energy that would have dissolved my body had it been present. My present-self did not know what to think. While Lao

Tzen continued to be overwhelmed by this flood of emotion that I too was experiencing through his eyes, I had no framework from which to comprehend what was happening. How was it possible that the feelings I had in the presence of Jesus could be had by someone in another religion? And how and why was I seeing this person as me? What was God trying to show me? However, the experience I was in was too intense for me to place any real attention on these questions. I simply continued to observe in utter fascination.

"Lao Tzen," my Master said to me. This was not the name of a stranger – it was my name. It was deep and personal. It contained within it an expression of the energy in my Master that was also within me. It was love itself and revelation of the highest and most beautiful kind. It was said with the same feeling that I felt from Jesus's lips when he spoke to me, "Brent."

I do not remember all that was spoken – only fragments. The conversation was also spoken in a way that defies language. While I could swear that Lao Tzen was both speaking and hearing in Mandarin, I understood the conversation as though it were in English. This was similar to an experience I had in Brazil once as a missionary. When one of my spiritual leaders spoke to the missionaries who were present, I was overcome with tears from the intensity of what I heard in that moment. I could not stop crying the whole night. The next day when I asked the Brazilian missionaries about it, they heard everything I did, only they swore it was spoken in Portuguese. Each of us heard in our own language, perhaps because it was no longer human language that was teaching us.

"Lao Tzen," my Master spoke again. "You must let me go."

Shock. Pain. Pure pain. He was my everything. "Master, never!"

"Lao Tzen – you must."

"But why?" I pled. This instruction to Lao Tzen had the same impact as I might have felt if Jesus asked present-day me to let go of Him. It was heart-breakingly unbearable.

"You cannot progress if you hold onto me," he answered.

As Lao Tzen, my mind was opened to see. As I have said before, "see" is probably the wrong word. However, there was an understanding so deep that it was visual. I felt eternities of possible joy open. I could see the progression from one lifetime to another. I saw how the devotion to my Master that had been so precious to me during life would affect other lifetimes being played out. It was as if I contemplated lives and experiences in other realms and saw that those lives would not bloom fully in their proper time if I was still clinging to him. My faith had lifted me, but my relationship to that faith would become an anchor if I did not let it go.

More bizarre, however, was that Lao Tzen's Master seemed to be performing a feat in which he was speaking dual meaning to both parts of me, past and present. While he spoke to Lao Tzen exclusively, I could not help but feel he was aware of the present-day part of me that was peaking in on this intimate scene. I am reminded of a scene in Harry Potter Chamber of Secrets where Harry was invisible to those present. Somehow, the headmaster, Dumbledore, knew he was there anyway and surreptitiously spoke to Harry by saying some words with dual meaning. The emphasis on the words made it clear to Harry that the message was meant for him. In this situation, my present self was like an invisible bystander, but I could feel the words as though they were spoken for my benefit. The Master was not just speaking to Lao Tzen, he was speaking to the part of Brent that was still Lao Tzen. Somehow, my progression in this life was conditioned in part on Lao Tzen truly releasing and letting go of his understanding of God and heaven.

As Lao Tzen, I wept and wept. I did not think there was any way I could force my heart to open, to relinquish its grip on the One who so lovingly and intimately connected me with the Divine. It was unbearable, but I finally was able to open my heart just a crack.

In precisely that moment, another nodal point of intelligent light came into me that felt like a higher branch from the first one, as though it were connecting me to an awareness of even more lifetimes. I was instantly transported into another set of memories. This time, I was in a lifetime where I had been a devoted disciple of Jesus. I lived in some period a hundred or two hundred years after the death of Jesus. Again, I felt the experiences not as separate from me, but as my own.

As I saw the devotion of this past-self through his eyes, I simultaneously became aware that there were a series of other memories from other lifetimes that could be brought to the surface for each major religious path. I had been in them all. I had learned from them all. I had found joy and beauty in each approach to understanding God.

Now suddenly, I was face to face with Jesus. The rush of joy in being in his presence was almost immediately eclipsed by heartbreaking pain when he asked me to do exactly what Lao Tzen had just gone through.

"You must let go," Jesus said.

He had just said the unthinkable for someone who fully embraced that he was "the way, the truth, and the life."[21] With his invitation to me, I almost snapped out of the spiritual experience. The pain in my present self was too much. As with Lao Tzen's master, Jesus was aware that he was speaking to both my past and present self. Only in this instance, Jesus seemed to be focused on the part of me in the present – this instruction was deeply personal and penetrated every part of me.

Perhaps, this invitation caught me so off guard because I never truly understood what the salvation of Jesus meant. Like so many other Christians, my reverence for him almost completely blinded me to his plain message for deep transformation of this life: "Beloved, now are we the sons of God, and it doth not yet appear what we shall be: but we know that, when he (Jesus) shall appear, we shall be like him; for we shall see him as he is."[22] The salvation he offered, beyond any futuristic release from the hell-like torment of the mind, was centered around the heart-felt,

---

[21] John 14:6

[22] 1 John 3:2

innermost experience of what it means that each of us are like him, that we are actually created in the image of God – not on how lowly or different we are from Jesus. The bridge he built between us and God was in showing us the roadmap of our human potential, of all that we might become, not in some supposed revelation of our deficiency. We receive that bridge when we allow the revelation of our sameness with him to unfold within us. The question then becomes, what is in him that is also in us, that when it is revealed we will see that we have always been like him? Clearly, there is an understanding to be given that most of us do not now possess or even know is possible.

I had spent so much time thinking about the future salvation of Jesus that it never occurred to me that I could receive it, not as some future inheritance, but as an actual possibility of awakening and deep transformation in this life. Like so many other Christians, I had become so immersed in the popular interpretation of the Bible that I could not hear his voice in the moment thereof inviting me to deeper understanding. For me, centuries of cultural interpretation buried the fuller invitation of Jesus so deep that I almost could not hear it. Even after seeing God, I still clung to my cultural understandings of Jesus rather than receiving the truth that would set me free.[23] The very church teachings that once pointed me to him now obscured my view. Like the cast that must come off when the bone is healed, so too must the rigidity of the cultural understandings and practices be released when we have healed enough to hear. It is not that the popular understanding of Jesus's message commonly taught in churches is bad or wrong; it is simply a different phase of growth. What a caterpillar needs to grow is not the same as a butterfly. Once it leaves the cocoon, the butterfly must learn to consume nectar instead of leaves or it will never truly fly. For just a moment, consider what is the spiritual nourishment you need to grow now? Is it the same as what you felt a few years ago? If not, how has it changed?

---

[23] "And ye shall know the truth, and the truth shall make you free." John 8:32

I spent many years studying Jesus's words in the Bible, but what I thought I knew about those words was what was holding me back. This is similar to a story I once heard about two men who died and went to be judged before entering heaven. The first was asked by the interviewer what he knew about Jesus, so he spent the next several hours almost repeating the Bible back word for word. Confident of his success, the first man left the room. Then the second man entered and before the interviewer could even ask a question, he fell to his knees weeping at the feet of the interviewer, crying out, "Jesus!" When we are stuck on what we think we know, sometimes we cannot see what is plainly in front of us. I cannot say how many times as a scientist that the very models that helped me to invent new DNA constructs then later blinded me to the next invention. The assumptions that made those models so effective at first, later prevented me from seeing anything more. *The model or understanding we use to approach God today frequently becomes the prison of our potential tomorrow.*

This transition of understanding can also be compared to an experience I had as a graduate student. One day, my thesis advisor told me it was time to let him go. I had only been in the program for two-and-a-half years, not nearly long enough to learn all that I needed to know, but he saw something I could not: he knew that I could never finish my education to become like him if I did not step out from underneath his shadow. The purpose of his teaching was not to keep me as his student forever, but to help me see as he saw, to understand as he understood. I had learned all I could as his "disciple." He would always have a special place in my heart for the role he played in my education, but to finish my education in becoming like him I needed to learn beside him as an equal. The undergraduate never rises above his/her teacher, but the true path of mastery in graduate school is to see and know as the teacher sees and knows. Therefore, the invitation to let go of our teacher is not a failure, but a deeply joyful and lifelong calling to experience through our own eyes the understanding that our teacher has. It is the path of the master. In inviting me to let go of him, Jesus wanted me to take the next step in my education to discover the revelation he came to give, that what was in his heart was also in mine.

Still, with the mindset I had at the time, I was not sure I could make my heart let go until the memory came back of what Lao Tzen learned with his Master. I had a spiritual awareness even through the pain that Lao Tzen's faith was preparation for what I now experienced with Jesus. I had to witness Lao Tzen and comprehend him in order to know what I must do now. I also knew from Lao Tzen's experience that I only needed my heart to open just a crack. It was enough to allow the light of change to enter in and open me to a new process. Though it seemed impossible, I moved into the space of surrender and created just the tiniest space or feeling of letting go.

As happened before, another nodal point of light entered, and I was instantly transported into another time period and another life time. This time I appeared to be in India. I was in the body of an Indian who had just had an avataric download, that is a revelation of being the light descended into human form in order to awaken humanity. I could still feel the understanding flowing through me of being the Light in all things and through all things. It was blissful beyond measure. In a way that was similar to how Lao Tzen felt in his Master's presence, and how I felt in Jesus's presence, the experience of total unity with All That Is was also blissful and filled with a feeling of salvation. Only in this case, it was also filled with an awe and wonder that had not been present previously. Rather than being an individual kneeling at the feet of the Master, it was the experience of enlightenment within the Master. It was oneness with all of creation and a full download of all understanding, yet in a way that was impossible to grasp fully with the finite mind. It simply resulted in incalculable joy.

As I felt this experience of unity with all of creation, I understood why Lao Tzen's master and then Jesus had asked me to let go of them. There was a difference between the light of which they were a fullness and the cultural traditions that had been built up around them. Somehow, in the centuries of academic tradition that followed Jesus's death and resurrection, Christianity had begun to use Jesus and his teachings as a means to emphasize our unworthiness of the light in this life rather than as a revelation of our potential evolution in the here and now. The resulting blindness that exists not only in Christianity but in the majority of world religions, helped maintain the veil between us and the knowledge of God until it was time for humanity to collectively wake up. This means that countless generations used their faith to "endure to the end" with hope in the hereafter until the time was ripe for humanity as a whole to undergo the type of transformation that was the real potential of this life. Our generation has the invitation to see and understand as the spiritual masters saw, in a way that awakens the comprehension of God in all creation in an explosion of overwhelming bliss, love, and light. It is time for us to receive salvation in the flesh and not just talk about it as a future inheritance. No other person, no matter how loving or worthy, can ever experience salvation in our behalf. To be heaven, we must experience that joy-beyond-comprehension for ourselves. That means the path to our awakening is through the comprehension of the joy that is in Jesus and the other spiritual masters – to become like them. The day must eventually come when we let go of our mother and father in order to step into the world and understand for ourselves. So too with those who spiritually birthed us. The day inevitably comes, when if we are to know as they know, we must step from outside of their shadow.

This avataric download was not at all what my mortal mind or body might have expected. There was no sense of ego whatsoever, no sense of value from being the light. Rather, almost the opposite happened. With that knowledge was the awareness of what existed inside of every other human being, something so precious and sacred – the divine light of God Himself. I felt the overwhelming humility from realizing that the role of an awakened god-being in the flesh was as a catalyst for awakening the Divine from its slumber in the bodies of so many other trapped beings. That humility stemmed from the paradox that while I would appear to be lifted in my role, yet I knew who it was I was serving. They were the Light too, only they could not see it. The presence of that Light in them, whether they saw it or not, meant that they were a fullness of that Loving Intelligence that was even then overwhelming all that I was. In effect, I saw that God would come to me in the form of all these people, seeking the very awakening that I was receiving from Him. This emotion almost had more of an effect on me than the experience of unity itself. It was the irony of me as a spiritual beggar being raised up by the Giver of All who was Himself masquerading as a beggar seeking enlightenment; the One at whose feet I should kneel was kneeling at mine in the form of the people I was being sent to awaken. There could be no more humbling paradox. Those people who had suffered their whole lives felt they were lower than the dirt, but they were so many sleeping expressions of the Divine Being – not separate expressions, but a fullness of God. And it would be my role in that lifetime to serve the sleeping God.

As I sat in this overwhelming feeling of union with God and simultaneous humility for the role then in front of me, I noticed a woman in the room with me that I considered to be divine. She was present to confirm upon me the understanding that had just been given to me by heaven. It was her role to anoint me to my purpose in that lifetime and she did so with so much love and devotion. In fact, she could see the revelation I was receiving and it was causing her to weep as she anointed my head and my feet.

While I watched this play out, I realized that this woman was familiar. The memory of it brought me back to an awareness of my body. She was the same woman who was then performing my Reiki attunements in this life. And all the more profound, though neither she nor I had said a word during the entire process of receiving my attunements, she was weeping as though she could see everything I was seeing too. In fact, in tandem with my vision, she was crying and anointing my feet in precisely the same way as I saw in the vision. She had completely departed from the formality of the Reiki attunements in order to do what we were both seeing and experiencing in joint vision.

When she was done, all we could do was sit and look at each other, still not understanding what had just happened or what it meant. I finally asked, "Did you see that?"

"Yes," she responded while still crying. "I saw it all. I was there with you."

I had no basis from which to interpret these experiences. Through the eyes of three different individuals, I had seen that which was sacred to each one of them. I had seen God through the eyes of three people who had cultures different from my own. In each case, the experience of God was equally profound. These people were not me, at least not in any way my present-day self could understand. Why their experience had been shared with me in such a deep and intimate way, I was completely unsure. However, I felt that it was somehow meant to help answer the questions I had been asking about the different paths unto God.

Through my own eyes, I had seen three different paths unto God and been aware of even more. I had seen the sincerity of the experiences in their hearts, even though they may have come from different religious understandings than myself. I could only sit and ponder as the intensity of these sacred experiences washed over me. I could no longer deny that those of other religions had experiences of God that were every bit as beautiful as my own. For I had seen through their eyes or my eyes as the case may have been.

It was not until later that I was able to understand more of the meaning and purpose behind seeing some of these things. I received guidance as follows:

> *This sequence of events was given to you that you might understand. The love and devotion of each people of the earth (in their religious path) is as great as the love and devotion you have felt in this present life of yours. That which people esteem to be God, even if they call not the person by the name "God," is viewed with the same reverence as you see Christ. Therefore, you may know the seriousness of the devotion of each of the twelve paths.*

> *Those that choose to remain on the earth shall continue to grow with the path that they have united with. They shall see greater and greater purity in their*

own paths until they are capable of interacting with other faiths without conflict.

At this point, some individuals will continue to progress by seeing what is beautiful, noble and virtuous in the other paths. It is in the uniting of the virtues of all the paths that one sees the true light and understanding of the heavens. For each path is but a type and a shadow of a deeper understanding. The truth lies in between these paths in the same way that you now see types and shadows in the religions of the world. The words can never hold heaven any more than the religions themselves can hold heaven. Rather, by seeing the strengths of each path and the weaknesses, the adherents of each can come to a greater understanding of that which can only be seen and experienced.

This path of progression is part of a greater path of enlightenment. As the various world faiths come together under one umbrella with sufficient purity so as to be able to appreciate the others and learn from the others, then there is a transformation wrought. These peoples are able to join hands and pray together, first with those from their own gates or paths. Then they are able to unite with each other, one person from each respective path. When all paths are united, the hearts are truly open to God and that which is symbolized in the creation circle is complete.

I understood that each religion held important truths. While they may all be looking for the same light we call God, yet their experience of that light was unique. Only by combining each of those sacred understandings and experiences could the full picture of God begin to emerge. I saw that there were many in this generation who would feel that same pull to awaken fully as the light and labor to unite all truth into one great whole. We would be able to respect each other from our respective backgrounds free from any judgment. In fact, it would give us great joy in learning how others had come to know and see the same light despite coming from different backgrounds.

Part 4

Twelve Fruits on the Tree of Life

Chapter 12

The Girl Who Could See without Eyes

The visions I had in my third experience created an entirely new way of looking at life for me. I could no longer consider that there was only one way of arriving in God's presence. The traditional Christian view that there is only one way to heaven was simply not supported by what I was being shown by Jesus. I had seen and even experienced through others' eyes the joy that came from the faith of other religious traditions. It seemed that the straight and narrow path to heaven,[24] rather than being defined by any one religion, had more to do with the sincerity and authenticity of devotion in an individual's heart regardless of their religious path. I had felt the love of God in each of these devoted individual's hearts – and it was that love that was precious above all else, not the paths they had chosen. This was reminiscent of the principle God showed me nearly twenty years earlier at the time of my baptism but had somehow forgotten – that the "true church" was not a single organization or doctrine, rather the people from all paths in whose hearts the love of God was truly found.

While I had started the journey into energy healing to learn new tools to help raise the earth, I now realized I was being led to an understanding of more than just tools. I was being taught something about the path each person takes to find God, the sacredness of that choice, and the love that God has for each of us in our chosen paths. Heaven truly was bigger than I had ever imagined. It caused me to open my eyes and wonder what understandings of God existed in the traditions of others that I

---

[24] "Enter ye in at the strait gate: for wide is the gate, and broad is the way, that leadeth to destruction, and many there be which go in thereat: Because strait is the gate, and narrow is the way, which leadeth unto life, and few there be that find it." Matthew 7:13-14

had not yet considered and how those understandings could enlarge my own.

To think, I had started my journey toward God out of fear, but now the fear had been replaced with a sense of wonder and curiosity. Once fear was gone, the innocence and wonder of a little child emerged. I wanted to learn everything about the way other cultures thought and believed. I wanted to understand their experience of God. Clearly, whatever I had believed about God was insufficient to capture the full understanding. God was so much more than anything I had imagined or anything I had understood from my religious tradition. Now, the question was, how much more was there to understand? What truths were contained in the other religious paths? I was embarking on a direction in my life where I truly had no idea what was going to happen next. It felt liberating and exhilarating to think where it might lead. As I continued to let go of my fear-bound restraints, where would Jesus lead me next?

As a way of showing God my willingness to take the next step regardless of where it led, I decided to close the previous chapter of my life by memorializing the learning I had acquired up to that point. I wrote a book about the connection between faith, healing, ascension, manifestation, and the subconscious programs inside of each of us. Among other things, I wanted to document the tools I had discovered for accessing and changing the subconscious programming that led to the faith to produce miracles. If it was possible that what I had already been through could help someone else, then I wanted to leave a few notes behind about the journey. *Faith to Produce Miracles* would be a workbook or a "how-to" book on developing truly transformative faith.

When I finished *Faith to Produce Miracles*, my excitement increased. "Father," I prayed. "I finished the book. I've let go of what has been, and I'm ready for my next teacher." I didn't just pray with words. I knew by then to see what I wanted in my heart and more importantly to *feel* it as if it was already done. This was what God had been teaching me to do to create new experiences and opportunities. That way, the feeling would go out into the light and the new experience would be brought back to me even as I had envisioned it.

Just like how we can change our emotions by remembering our saddest or happiest moments, I prepared my being to change my emotional state, to allow a new emotion into my space. I could feel the expansion of my soul, the way it would feel to be embraced by new knowledge, learning, and opportunities. I could feel the satisfaction of having been led to a teacher that was divinely appointed for the next phase of my learning. This feeling was more than just a passing emotion of attachment, the way that we might long for a new car, or a house, or a significant other. It was not a feeling of desire fueled by any degree of lack, but rather, it was a feeling of healing and liberation that caused my heart to swell. I knew that was the emotion which brought back answers with power. And as I had been taught, I completely let go of what it would look like or how it would happen.

A week or so later, I was watching some videos on YouTube. I saw one of those sponsored videos on the side that I intentionally never click on and suddenly felt very strongly that I should. It was a video of a young Indian girl demonstrating the ability to read blindfolded. There were lots of comments afterwards of varying states of belief or incredulity. But I didn't care about their opinions. I had begun developing the ability to sense the emotions of others and I could feel the girl's sincerity. What's more, I knew that few young children were capable of shielding their true emotions.

As I watched with curiosity, I felt the presence of Jesus near me. He said something to me that surprised me, even after all I had seen. "Find who taught this girl to do this and go there."

I was a little bit startled. This girl was obviously Hindu. Despite the fact that I was opening to new experience, I still found it ironic in a way that made me laugh that Jesus would send me to a Hindu ashram. Nevertheless, I recognized the fulfillment of my heart's manifestation. The fact that this answer was so far outside of my previous experience almost made it more exciting.

It didn't take me long to find the girl's teacher, Swami Nithyananda, located at a Hindu ashram in Bidadi, India. I discovered that the ashram was hosting a twenty-one-day retreat for visitors the next month. In what appeared to me to be divine synchronicity, we had also just received an unexpected sum of money that would cover the full cost of the retreat along with travel. It seemed to Jenn and I to be confirmation of the direction I had received. So, I booked the trip. A month later, I flew into Bangalore, India, the closest major airport to Bidadi.

Chapter 13

Understanding the Grace of Jesus at a Hindu Ashram

The first day at the ashram was a beautiful experience for me. It was like walking through a door into a whole new experience in this life that somehow simultaneously felt like coming home, as though to a home on high that I had temporarily forgotten in this life. There was an ache in my heart that felt relieved, as if to remember something so important that had disappeared from my awareness for a time. That feeling was connected to a distinct frequency of light I felt in the area around the ashram. It was tangible to me in the same way I felt in the temple shortly after I was baptized. Only, this was a different frequency. It wasn't that same feeling of light and holiness I associated with the Christian Father, Son, and Holy Ghost. Rather, it was a feeling of enlightenment, joy, and causeless bliss. It felt like laughter for no reason – spontaneous joy without a cause. It felt so amazingly good, like awakening a part of me that had long been asleep, that was overjoyed to find itself awake again. I wondered at how I could be in such a foreign place among people who looked and acted so differently than myself and yet feel so at home.

That first day, I admit to behaving a little like a tourist. I wanted to take pictures of everything. At one point, I was taking pictures of some of the Hindu children dressed in orange robes. Suddenly, I heard a voice with a thick Indian accent in my heart and mind saying, "Brent, it is not appropriate for you to take pictures here."

I looked around sharply. Although I was accustomed to frequently hearing voices from the other side, this one was new. I recognize the voice of Jesus, but I had never heard this voice before. Who was it that had spoken to me?

I did not have long to ponder, however, because some of the orange-robed adult renunciates (sannyasi) approached to tell me that we were in a holy place and that we should not be taking pictures. I put my camera away and went on with our first-day tour of the ashram.

It was not until later in the day that I finally discovered who had been speaking to me. We were brought to a place where we could hear Swamiji (the tender epithet given to Swami Nithyananda by his disciples) speak. I stopped with a great degree of surprise – his voice was the same voice that had spoken in my heart and mind! But how was that possible for a living person to do?

Perhaps if I had better understood how Hindus see their gurus, it would not have been so difficult for me to understand. They see gurus as divine beings and worship them as such. While that may have previously seemed like superstition to me, yet when Hindus have near-death experiences, they often encounter their guru in the same way that I saw Jesus in my experiences. As it turned out, there were those at the ashram who had seen Swamiji during their own near-death experiences.

Since I was at Swamiji's ashram, it should not have surprised me too much that it would be Swamiji speaking in my heart and mind. I was just unaware that his spiritual presence could be so cognizant of visitors in remote places of the ashram.

It took me some time to get used to his voice speaking to me. Him telling me to put my camera away would not be the last time he spoke to me. In fact, while I was at the ashram, his voice became a near constant for me. I even had to take some time apart to ask Jesus whether it was ok that someone living was so present in my heart and mind! Jesus's response to me was that he had brought me here to learn from Swamiji, so I should trust enough to allow this process to unfold.

Beyond hearing Swamiji's voice in my mind and heart, that first day was amazing. For those who have never been to India, it is a remarkably vibrant place. The clothing is very rich and full of color. The rituals of Hinduism are especially full of colors that seem lost to much of the rest of the world. Even the orange robes of the sannyasi have a certain beauty as they cover the tanned skin of Indians who have their hair woven in thick dreadlocks, or jaatas, as they are called in India.

When Hindus of certain faiths take the vows of the renunciate, they shave their heads, including their beards and eyebrows. After shaving their head, they allow the hair to grow back and do not cut it again. The length of the hair becomes an indication of the length of discipleship. The jaatas are signs of renunciation and the release of concern over physical vanity.

What surprised me the most that first day is the openness those at the ashram had in sharing with us spiritual gifts. In my religion, we saw spiritual gifts, revelations, and the like as extremely sacred. They were not to be shared and were to be kept for our personal edification. Yet, those at the ashram shared their gifts openly. They wanted all to "come and see."[25]

More amazing to me though was that they sent their children out to teach us. Instead of sending the older devotees, children between eight and sixteen years of age showed us the spiritual gifts that were being manifest in the ashram. We were told later that this was to help us believe that the same spiritual manifestations in them could be present in us too. In other words, if we saw children doing it, then our adult vanity would tell us we should be able to do it as well.

We watched that afternoon as children rolled coconuts without touching them by intention alone, read blindfolded, psychically diagnosed disease in members of our group, and remotely visited our homes in faraway places allowing them to describe unique details that they could not have known unless they had been there. One of the devotees also demonstrated the materialization of matter, similar to Jesus multiplying the loaves and the fishes in the Biblical story.[26] Only in this case, the devotee produced sacred Hindu relics, such as small golden coins, out of thin air.

---

[25] John 1:39

[26] Matthew 14:15-21

Just because I had been spiritually led to this ashram did not mean that I closed my eyes to other explanations for what we were seeing. I stayed open to the possibility that not all that appeared to be a miracle was actually a miracle. But as the weeks went on and we had direct interaction with the children at the ashram, I realized that they may have different religious understandings from my own, but they are very sincere. They are just as sincere with their spiritual pursuits as I am with my own. Their faith is so great that they have more of the miraculous signs that are supposed to attend the followers of Christ than many Christians do.[27] In other words, I witnessed so many real demonstrations of spiritual gifts and I saw such sincerity in those present that I do not believe them capable of conscious deception. I believe we were really witnessing multiple spiritual gifts, things most of us would call miracles.

They went on to discuss other gifts that we did not see, such as teleporting small objects. They discussed with great joy their hopes that one day instead of moving small objects, they would be moving people.

The openness with which they shared their spiritual gifts was a new experience for me. My religious culture encouraged those who could work miracles or see visions to keep them to themselves, lest their egos start to block the light of God for others. However, what I saw at the ashram was the opposite. They were encouraged to share their gifts and experiences so that more people could see the light. Those at the ashram did not believe that the ego could produce or maintain spiritual gifts. Rather, spiritual power only manifests when there is oneness with God. Since manifesting spiritual power in front of others is often perceived to be more difficult by most of us (e.g. due to the pressure and stress that arise from trying to "perform" or the possibility of getting it "wrong"), it was an opportunity for greater oneness with God to use the gifts in front of others. You had to be in a much greater state of allowing grace in order to

---

[27] Mark 16:17-18

manifest spiritual power in front of others than you did if you were on your own. Truly like Jesus's teaching that "a city that is set on an hill cannot be hid,"[28] the Hindus at Swamiji's ashram believed in setting their light upon the hill for all to see.

Later that day we were already initiated into the power of moving matter with our hearts. I say we were doing it with our hearts, because some people misunderstand the idea of moving matter with their minds. Moving matter is not a function of mental exertion. It in no way resembles the semblance of mental constipation, or pushing and shoving with the mind, frequently seen in those who do telekinesis in the movies. Actually, it is quite the opposite. It involves releasing all the force we unconsciously place upon the object we are witnessing. It is akin to unobserving, or a process of allowing the object to be more than what countless generations of experience tell us it should be. Without even thinking about it, the moment we see something, we define it. In the definition come the limitations of its height, depth, width, and how it acts. To move the object with the heart is to let go of those unconscious definitions. It is a function of absolute trust and surrender. It is the trust that God has no limits and not only can do it but is loving enough to fulfill our every need and request that we make from a space of unity.

The coconut moved not when I exerted force with my mind upon it, but when I ceased to exert all force upon it. Ironically, the force that I had to let go of was the force I was not even aware I was exerting. The observation of the coconut in accordance with thousands of years of past human observation prevents the coconut from ever being anything more than a coconut. The force that is applied is our conditioned acceptance of humanity's observations of possibility, or in this case, the lack thereof.

There is a space within us when we release the coconut or any other object or experience from all force. We allow it to exist as awareness rather than a physical construct defined in a physical world. The capacity for consciousness to recognize itself allows

---

[28] Matthew 5:14-16

the properties of the physical world to become more fluid in nature, which is the path to expansion and growth. This is the boundary between the physical and the spiritual, the space where spiritual potential can manifest in physical form. The coconut can suddenly roll where it otherwise would not.

I learned a valuable lesson about the structure of reality while considering the symbol of moving the coconut. The complexity of human awareness that separates us from the continuous acknowledgement of God is not physical. That is, it is not rigidly fixed and unchangeable the way we might suppose. It only feels like an impenetrable wall because we do not know that the wall of thought and emotion that appears to separate us is not us. Our whole lives, we have lived with the programs we were given by our parents and society around us. These include a list of what we should and should not do, what is real and what is not real.

The coconut then is a symbol for all other healing that takes place. Every obstacle in our physical world is not what it appears to be. Relationships, finances, and other heartache break down into walls of emotion that often cause us to feel broken, defeated, or powerless. Many of these emotions seem to be immovable precisely because they appear to be fixed parts of our identity. However, when we release the force of subconscious thought that holds them in a fixed pattern, we can experience all of it as light and awareness. From the space of awareness, that which was immovable can suddenly change – can suddenly heal for ourselves and countless generations before us. Where the internal structure changes, the outer world often follows with remarkable precision. This is inner world healing for outer world results. The barriers that have been unbreakable in our lives can move in an instant.

Since we were never taught a technique to do this, only given demonstrations, perhaps it should come as no surprise that our group struggled at times to understand the concept. So, one member of our group asked Swamiji for a technique to help us, "If you could just give us a technique, then we could do it."

"There is no technique. All technique is for the guru. It is for the guru to teach you that you can't do it. It is all grace," Swamiji replied.

That principle profoundly impacted me. I had spent the whole of my adult life trying to measure up for grace. This concept went far beyond just the idea of religious salvation. My insistence that I needed to do my part actually handicapped my faith in every part of my life. I saw that unless I had done "all I can do," then I had no faith that the miracle could happen. Not only that, but it became clear that "all I can do" was not even clearly defined. So, I never actually hit that imaginary standard, no matter how hard I tried, because I always believed I could do more before God would intervene. Even in the instances where I had felt God's help in the past, I saw clearly it only came once I hit the point of complete failure. It was at that precise moment when I would finally give up and go to God with actual faith that He would help. In the past, it took me doing all I could do before grace was manifest because I needed to do everything to finally see that none of my efforts would work and to finally let go. Faith was in the surrender, not in my efforts. It was always grace.

This understanding created a sudden moment of insight and liberation – if it was always grace, then the power to work the miracle could come forth at any moment or any time. I did not have to wait for the trial of my faith or until failure the way I had done in the past. All that needed to happen was for me to stop using my beliefs to limit my faith of what God would or would not do in this moment. I needed to open to the possibility that God was truly love and that all my heart's desires were manifest through grace, not through any effort or worthiness of my own.

To think that I had misunderstood the principle of grace almost my entire adult life! All too often, people in western cultures feel that they need to somehow earn God's love just as people in eastern cultures feel they need to follow a process to achieve enlightenment. Each religion, each philosophy dictates the path to qualifying for that love. And yet I finally understood – in the end, each of those paths is not what leads us to God, they are the technique given to teach us that we can never earn God's love or acceptance. We can only surrender and finally allow him to shower us with a love that is given without price or condition.

I saw the irony in my past attempts to change my behavior. The force I used internally to create the change in my behavior to be "good" ironically deprived me of the very experience of God's love in the present moment that I needed to have real change. Suppression of undesirable thoughts and behavior just led to pain. In contrast, understanding and awareness led to healing of inner hurts in a way that caused the behavior to actually change from the heart. The religious technique I had been given was so that I could realize that none of it could ever return me to the presence of God, to that foundational awareness that filled me with the joy of heaven. My whole approach was backward. It was always grace.

It was ironic to me that I never truly understood the Christian principle of grace until I visited a Hindu ashram and studied with a Hindu guru. But indeed, it was through grace that all spiritual power manifested during our three weeks at the ashram.

Not only that, but I soon learned that the grace needed to move the coconut was the same needed to move the fear, guilt, and shame within our hearts that create the veil between us and the experience of God's love in the present moment. Each of these anchoring emotions was like a coconut that I was completely powerless to move until I surrendered and God took over. The hurts and fears within my subconscious that prevented me from letting go and allowing the manifestation of spiritual power were just as physical in some sense as the coconut. I was just as powerless to move them. I only needed to allow God to bring them to my attention and then to surrender into light, allowing him to move and release these patterns. In this way, my growth would continue in the way that it was meant to.

During the days that followed, frequently I would hear Swamiji's voice in my heart and mind coaching me through what was blocking me in manifesting spiritual gifts. He would point out the roots of beliefs and childhood trauma deep within my subconscious. Then, as I would start to use the energy-healing and other techniques I had learned over the years to move them, he would ask me, "Why can't you just let God do this? Why can't you simply accept grace?"

I realized what he meant. Not only was I always trying to fix myself, I was trying to fix those around me. After all the time and money I spent on learning energy healing and other forms of subconscious work, I had a lot of value tied up in my ability to help others. I could see the subconscious blocks of those around me and would try to intervene to fix them, and again I would hear Swamiji's voice, "Just allow grace." Analyzing subconscious limitations under a microscope or flowing energy were just stepping stones to a deeper principle where awareness simply met allowance. I was to learn something entirely new – how to completely let go and let God take over, not just for me, but for the whole world around me as well. In a broader context, it was also a lifting of the burden from the responsibility to purify my heart so that the world might be raised. None of us individually ever had the power to lift or transition the earth. If it is to happen, it will be by grace and our release into the joy where it is already done – through our allowance of grace in the release of the need to do it.

I remember my first time in the temple of my religion. There was such a beautiful feeling of peace throughout the entire building. And yet, as I would move into the most sacred places within the temple, the worst thoughts that could possibly come into my mind would arise. I used to crucify myself that I could have these thoughts in a place I felt so much reverence for.

At first, I thought I was being punished. Since my view of God and the world at that time was that God punished the wicked, it only made sense that this is how I would see things. And yet, over time I finally came to realize that the thoughts that were brought up were not to punish me, but for me to see so that God could finally heal them. I was not expected to do anything, except to trust and allow. That which is in darkness (e.g. outside of our awareness) must be brought to light in order to heal.

Now here in the ashram, that lesson came fully to the forefront of my mind. All of these blocks exist within us that separate us from the moment-to-moment experience of the divine space. We are no less divine here upon the earth than we were in the state before this life. It is only the beliefs which are deep within the subconscious space of our bodies that manifest conditions that cause us to appear separate from God.

These beliefs arising in connection with the physical body have an element of physicality. Perhaps we do not consider them physical because we cannot see them with our eyes or touch them with our hands, but at some level of reality, they are physical. Every belief and emotion literally have physical representations in our brains. There is a chemical or hormone connected to each emotion. There is a neural pathway for each belief. There is a set of genes which have been up or down regulated as a result of these internal chemical communications. And therefore, there is a unique physical expression in our bodies that is a direct or indirect result of these beliefs and emotions.

Just as changing physical disease seems beyond us at times, so too is changing the underlying beliefs and emotions responsible for the expression of our physical body beyond us. To change any part of our divinely-orchestrated make up or expression, we need the loving intervention of the divine. So it was that I learned grace at a deeper level. I learned how to let go and how to surrender.

Chapter 14

The Problem with Our Eyes

"No, that isn't what you saw," the woman said in a thick Indian accent. She was directing her comment to one of the men in our group. He was trying to tell her that he did not have the ability to remotely view another person's home using his mind's eye because nothing he saw was correct.

She continued, "That is the meaning you added to what you saw. Don't interpret what you are seeing, just see. When you can learn to see without adding your own story to it, then you will be seeing what truly is."

Our group stood looking at the woman in some amazement. The man never told her what he saw. Even so, she described to him in perfect, vivid detail what he had seen in addition to the subconscious beliefs that had created his interpretation.

Like so many of us, the man thought he was seeing, but what he was really doing was unknowingly telling a story about what he saw. His own story and his unconsciousness to it blinded him to what was really there.

Now it was my turn. My partner's name was Puresh. I knew nothing about him other than we were part of the same group, and I was supposed to go into his home in my mind's eye and describe what I saw. Of course, after what we just heard, I now had a focus – don't add a story, just describe what I see.

As my mind went quiet, the first images starting coming. I saw something that looked blue and rectangular. As I looked harder it came into focus. It was the blue police box that serves as Dr. Who's time machine called the Tardis.

What? That can't be right! I thought. *Maybe, it means he lives in the UK because that's where Dr. Who is filmed. Wait, I'm not supposed to interpret. Just write down "Tardis" and keep going before you freeze up.* More images came. I saw a room with a couch with the ocean and sailboats above it.

"Time!" the woman called out. "Tell your partner exactly what you saw. Don't leave out any details."

Great, I thought. *What are the chances he lives in a Tardis? Here goes nothing.*

"I saw Dr. Who's Tardis," I said, cringing as I waited for laughter and a statement of how ridiculous that was.

"No way!" he exclaimed. "My daughter has a full-size Tardis in her bedroom. How on earth did you see that?"

I couldn't believe it. How in the world did that just line up? It gave me confidence to continue.

"I saw a couch underneath a picture of the ocean with sailboats in it." I felt more confident about getting this one right. If the Tardis was right, then this better be spot on.

"Almost," he said. "I live in California right on the ocean. There's a window over the couch that looks out on the ocean where there are usually a bunch of sailboats."

The woman was looking at me intently. "You didn't see a picture," she said. "That is the story your mind added to it. If you just told what you saw, a couch with the ocean and sailboats above it, it would have been exactly right. Learn the difference between what you think you are seeing and what actually is. Do not add your story to what the divine is revealing to you."

As I reflected on what I saw, I realized she was right. The images of the ocean and sailboats I saw in my mind were not labeled "picture." I just assumed it was a picture. On closer inspection, I could see the assumption happened so quickly that I didn't even notice it was a substitute for reality until my attention was called to it. My mind simply gave me the assumption as if it *were* reality. In hindsight, I could see how my mind was altering what I thought I saw in every moment, almost without any trace of its tampering. It was as if my mind was incapable of communicating to me without trying to weave a narrative from the experiences.

The irony about seeing is that sometimes we think that because we see, we understand. Yet, it is the belief that we know what we see that causes us to fail to truly see. It prevents us from analyzing and seeing the projection of our minds upon our experience, which in turn keeps us from grasping understanding beyond the bounds of our past narratives. This is a similar concept to what Jesus taught the respected religious leaders in his day. It was because of what they thought they "saw" that prevented them from finding deeper understanding and being healed.[29] In each moment, we are fabricating a story around what we are seeing instead of seeing what truly is.

Since that recognition, I've often wondered, out of those who have seen God in near-death experiences and visions, how many of them have actually *seen*? How many were blinded by their own subconscious narratives? Is it even possible to see God without adding some kind of interpretation? Is the story and the meaning we ascribe to it fundamentally part of what it means to be human?

What I and others returned with from the other side is beautiful. But none of us returned with just the experience. Rather, we returned with the story we have attached to the small part of what we actually remember of what we experienced. The story is like a translation from the language of God into the limited language of human consciousness we currently reside in.

This is one reason why the stories of those who have seen the other side do not always match. One is that heaven is bigger than most people realize, but the other is that people are interpreting their experiences through their own subconscious narrative. By virtue of the editing being a subconscious process, they never even realize they are doing it. To them, the story they have woven is synonymous with the experience. They are not seeing what truly is; rather, they are seeing the experience as it exists through a filter.

---

[29] "And some of the Pharisees which were with him heard these words, and said unto him, Are we blind also? Jesus said unto them, If ye were blind, ye should have no sin: but now ye say, We see; therefore your sin remaineth." (John 9:40-41)

153

This is like the individual who has colored glasses. Everything they see is in a shade of green, yellow, or red depending on the filter used. I have included a brief excerpt of a poem by Dana Parker and Hannah Foust on awakening to their own personal filters:

I was born wearing rose colored glasses.

The walls of my house?

They were painted to reflect what life should be

In broad strokes of should's and have-to's.

There just wasn't enough room for all of me.

I was asked to fit in to what had already been,

To all the secrets and hiding and one-way roads.

The rose-colored glasses promised love in return for obedience

And yet all I wanted was to be free.

Rose-colored glasses shattered in slow motion,

Eyes adjusting to a new reality, stinging and raw.

My heart that was wrung in the hands of loved ones,

My cotton-filled throat that was muted and muffled,

And a voice that can't travel through walls.

Reality altered in the span of few years,

A woman inside a cocoon.

This process a choice against comfort,

Private in nature and rare to endure.

The old life was dissected and questioned,

A foundation built on my own inner joy and intuition.

And heart swells became my compass,

Trading old filters for messy, creative exploration.

I became a sovereign woman when I stopped looking for others to hear the truth of my heart,

When I lovingly looked within my own being beyond the glimmering voices of the past;

It was the day the voice of God outshined the weight of tradition.

Whitewashing walls to make room for this heart's desires.

Unapologetically me, for all to see,

A woman taking flight on the most joy-filled, fulfilling, magic adventure.

Imagine going through life with such a filter and never realizing that you were wearing it. Everything you saw or experienced would be distorted. Each of us have those filters of which we are entirely ignorant. It is part of human nature. We see and experience God through a filter that provides a unique story. The uniqueness of that story is a big part of the type of experience we have with God. It is also a big part of the fruit we come to taste in His presence.

Chapter 15

Fourth Experience: The Light in All Heavens

Swamiji's eyes were deep oceans of peace. Even though I had met individuals in the past I considered to be "enlightened," his eyes were different. There was no trace of the individual subconscious patterns left of the ego-self he had been before. I could not see any remnants of a person. There was only an infinite expanse.

Perhaps the most remarkable part of being at the ashram was the chance to see a living person operating in that brainwave or that state of consciousness. Being empathic, I pick up on other people's emotional states. Every time I saw him, my body would become confused, almost as if the contradiction of near-infinite light in a finite body were impossible. It kept telling me that the state he occupied should not exist in a physical form. I could only stare.

As my body would see his, I would immediately enter into involuntary movements. I had felt this energy and movement before in one of my healings with Jesus, but I did not know what it was at the time. Now I had a reference for it, "kundalini." These movements and rushes of at times blissful energy up my spine felt more than physical to me. It felt like the intelligence within my body was repatterning based on the truths it was witnessing within this individual. There was a part of me that was both seeing and learning that was not my conscious mind. Another way of saying it is that the operating system governing the physical, mental, and emotional appearance of my body in the physical world was receiving a massive update. The result was manifested in physical form through movement of my body and the flow of blissful energy.

It was during one of these moments of spontaneous kundalini that a vision of the Hindu heavens opened for me. This was not a long or detailed vision – it did not need to be. I only needed to see that it existed. I needed to feel the joy of the frequency of light unique to Hinduism when it is fully manifested in a heavenly state.

Describing the internal world in a physical way is perhaps one of the most challenging exercises. When we describe a place we have visited in the physical world, it is easy to speak of it in terms of the colors, shapes, smells, sounds, and so on. There is a universally spoken language due to shared experience in our physical world that allows us to understand each other. However, when we journey into the inner worlds, experiences are incredibly subjective, comprised of features that do not fit into any of the five senses, and yet, are somehow larger than all of them. It is as if the five senses blind us more than they allow us to see. They are not even the tip of the iceberg in potential experience, they are more like the head of a needle stuck in the tip of the iceberg compared to what we can truly see and understand.

Therefore, even in a heavenly experience that lasts for just a few seconds, more understanding and expansion of awareness can be communicated than can be obtained in a lifetime of solitary study. Yet, because this understanding and awareness takes place in a realm that cannot be described with the five senses, most of it cannot be brought back into this world in a way that can be communicated to others with our words. It is something that has to be experienced personally.

Perhaps that is for the best, because it means none of us are ever limited to what someone else experienced. Each of us must experience heaven for ourselves, must comprehend God for ourselves, making salvation a truly unique and individualized experience. It is like being the only child of an entire universe expressly created to bring about your most intense and ever-lasting joy. Our experiences are never limited to what others have seen and heard or the arbitrary bounds that they have placed upon heaven.

The confusing part of trying to express these experiences is that we rely so heavily on sight in this world. Like I have expressed before, it is not my eyes that see in these experiences. It is an understanding, an awareness, an energy that is so expansive that it comprises an experience my mind can only interpret as sight. But how do I communicate that type of sight when the experience takes on colors or shapes or concepts for which we don't have an earthly analog? It is similar to when I have been asked to translate a word from Portuguese into English and thought – there really is no word in English for that concept! Instead, you are left with the confusing task of trying to express a concept for which there literally is no translation.

In that same way, I saw symbols and people. But they were not symbols or people – that is only the best language I have for it. What I was really seeing was understanding, it was awareness, it was expansion of consciousness. This wave of euphoria was like the envelopment of intimacy when we first enter into our lover or they enter into us – that sudden intake of breath. Only, instead of a wave of deep sexual bliss, it was a wave of euphoric ecstasy in deep union with the Divine Mind. It was ambrosia of the sweetest kind, a bliss of connection where every emotion elicited in the human mind by each sight, sound, smell, and understanding in Vedic traditions were suddenly amplified thousands or even millions of times. This wave of energetic bliss and euphoria carried with it an understanding of an eternity of deepening bliss in cosmic unity. All the sights, sounds, smells, experiences, etc. were compound into one, inviting me with as much bliss and possibly even more than what I had experienced in sacred joy in the presence of Jesus.

From my limited perspective, what I was "seeing" was so much more than what I had experienced with Jesus. Maybe that's the wrong way of saying it. It was not "more than" as if what I experienced with Jesus was less. It was just completely different. Sometimes when people say "different" they mean it with a negative slant or in a way that forces us to choose one as good and the other as bad. However, this difference wasn't that at all. It was more like awakening to the childhood home I had forgotten – the taste of warm milk, fresh pie, the love of mom – as though this were every bit as much my home as what I had experienced with Jesus. How confusing to the mind! Which heaven was my heaven when they both felt like an inseparable part of me?

As of yet, I still wasn't coming from the perspective that there were multiple heavens. I was coming from the understanding that there were multiple paths to the same heaven. I believed all heavens were the same. Why wouldn't I? The experience of heaven is so expanding that it leaves us believing that we have experienced all truth. We just never imagine that heaven could be so big that we could expand infinitely into different directions with equally joyful, but entirely different, experiences. However, now I knew the truth. There was not just more than one way to heaven, there was actually more than one heaven, or more than one direction in which consciousness could expand with infinite potential. In the expanded state of mind I was in, I intuitively knew that there were many, many such heavens – so many directions of expansion and eternal progression that to my mortal mind they were uncountable.

I might as well have been in an ice cream shop after years of only knowing and eating vanilla, and suddenly discovering the existence of chocolate. My paradigms were totally disrupted. Chocolate was good! Even beyond good, it was phenomenal! It didn't make vanilla any less wonderful, but how could I live my life without chocolate now that I knew it existed? If I could have felt anything other than unconditional love and awe, I might have felt torn between this place and my loyalty to the Christian heaven I had already experienced.

In fact, the beauty of this place was so great as to elicit the unconscious question, "Did I pick the wrong one?" I had seen the Christian heaven, but this was wonderful in a whole different way that my soul ached to experience. This thought ran through my being even while another part of me felt almost disloyal for having that thought. Since the existence of multiple unique heavens had never truly occurred to me before, perhaps it also makes sense that it never occurred to me that maybe I could have both – and maybe that was an even fuller comprehension of heaven. At this point, my feeling about finding another spiritual path attractive was tantamount to the sense of inner conflict people sometimes have at feeling deep or intimate connection with an individual other than their lawfully-wedded spouse. It was unexpectedly wonderful – but I felt the inner conflict of commitment to another! Jesus had given me permission to learn from other paths, but had he given me permission to have spontaneous orgasmic eruptions within another? Was it ok that I was asking the question whether I had made the right choice to be with him?

As these thoughts crossed through the background of my mind even while I looked upon the vision with a feeling of awe, I heard a voice speaking to me from the center of eternity. It said something to the effect of, "I am the Light in all things which includes the Light in all religions and through all heavens."

In that moment understanding came into my being – there truly is one God. Though we may worship a variety of deities in religions around the world, yet there is one light in them all and that one light is God. Though there might be thousands of heavens, yet that heaven which is greatest of all is the one in which all light from each of the heavens in all their glory is allowed free from any judgment, fear, guilt, or shame. It isn't just one flavor of ice cream; it is recognizing that you are an heir to the whole ice-cream store. All flavors are part of the highest.

After that vision I might have stayed in the ashram forever. It was beautiful. But heaven had not opened that vision for me to stay in a Hindu ashram. I was given that vision for understanding of the integration of all light into one great whole. I needed to know that the heavens of other religions were real and beautiful beyond compare. Still, the Hindu vision of the heavenly city brought down to earth is beautiful. They have a plan to achieve it. And I had now seen that the heavens of other religions and cultures are real. I had seen the beauty within them and had begun to suspect that the greatest heaven is not the one limited by culture and tradition, but the one that is open to all the light from all the heavens.

Chapter 16

The Brazilian Tree with Oranges and Lemons

A few weeks later, my friends John and Kristy asked me to stop by and discuss my experiences in India. Their curiosity went deeper than rolling coconuts or general questions about the culture. Instead, they were asking about my experience with the light in Hinduism and whether the faith of the Hindu's was as valid as our own. I searched for an analogy to help articulate my experience. A memory returned to me of something I had seen as a missionary in Brazil:

"Hey! Look at this," my missionary companion called to me. I was twenty-four at the time and we were in a typical, tropical backyard with abundant vegetation and fruit trees. But something was different about this one.

"Check it out!" he exclaimed. "There's a lemon on this branch and an orange on that one!"

I looked for myself. Sure enough. There were oranges on one branch, lemons on another, and other citrus varieties on the others – but all on the same tree! Even up close, they looked identical to the fruits on normal trees.

The property owner confirmed what we were seeing, "We grafted different citrus branches into the same root stock so it'll grow lemons and oranges. Go ahead and try one."

Eager to test out this strange tree, we discovered the oranges tasted like oranges, and "Uggh!" the lemons tasted like lemons. The tree was what it looked like, a single tree bearing multiple types of fruit.

As this memory surfaced, I thought about my friends' question about the Hindu light. I replied, "It's hard to explain. There was not only a completely different frequency of light than what I've experienced before, but the end spiritual fruit was different as well. However, different than we might have been taught or believed, I felt that this fruit was equally beautiful to the fruit at the end of our own spiritual path. I mean, it's like the tree of life has more than one fruit on it."

Kristy looked up sharply at me as if to see if the same light bulb that went off in her head had hit me too. Then she asked me a Biblical question taking my familiarity with the particular passage for granted, "When was the last time you read Revelation 22:2?"

Some of my friends really like repeating numbers. When they see three or more numbers in a row, it tickles them, as if the universe is somehow winking at them. I had that moment as she mentioned Revelation 22:2. While I was certainly amused by the play on numbers, I wasn't immediately familiar with the verse.

"It's been awhile," I responded.

"Revelation 22 is the last chapter in the book of Revelation," she began. "In it, John sees the celestial city. In verse 2, he describes the tree of life in the center of the city. And he says it 'bear twelve manner of fruits.' That's just like what you are describing!"

Was it possible? I had already considered that the twelve gates into Zion (the city of one heart and mind) represented twelve different paths. But now, it seemed like there was a unique fruit for each of the paths as well!

My mind was blown as I considered the implications. Ever since I had heard the parable of the six blind men and the elephant, I had considered that there were many paths leading to the same destination. Now for the first time, I realized that those paths actually led to quite different destinations. The experience of the ear of the elephant was vastly different than the experience of the leg. Each of these religions were teaching a unique path that led to a unique spiritual fruit and Revelation 22:2 described that!

"But what does that mean for all the religions?" I asked somewhat rhetorically. "Each thinks they have the only way to God, and I guess, they do in a way. It's like each has the only way to get to their particular fruit. But if that's true, then all of them belong in the city of light!"

Kristy built on my excitement, "Yeah! That's why none of them can succeed in building a true city of light. Each is trying to do it alone without the help of the others. But it was never meant to be that way – we were supposed to learn to work together!"

We just sat and looked at each other for a moment. Both of us knew many people who were very interested in building cities of light. Each had their own ideas about how it would be done. I personally had met individuals from multiple cultures who felt called to establish these communities.

Kristy was right, they were all trying to do it by gathering people who held identical beliefs to their own. No one was trying to figure out how to incorporate multiple viewpoints because each felt their own truth was the purest truth. Therefore, they each wanted a community of homogenous fellow believers.

But what would it take for these disparate groups of enlightened thinkers to start seeing and respecting each other? Beyond that, how could they ever reach the point where they truly wanted what the others were contributing in their communities? In the same way that a company might employ engineers, sales people, accountants, and others, each spiritual path has a complementary role to play in the big picture, even if they don't value the others. Were the cultural views that have divided us in the past too great?

I knew that each culture had built up walls against the others in order to retain their purity. Those walls were often rigidly reinforced with fear, guilt, and shame. Each viewed the other paths as misinformed, if not outright deceived. And there was almost always a type of spiritual pride connected with the idea of being part of the "true path" that contributed to the blindness to outside truths – just like the six blindmen who failed to see what the others were experiencing because they were blinded by the truth of their own experience of the elephant!

The impossibility of the task of reconciliation loomed large in my mind given the divide we have in our society over even the smallest of issues. Yet, I began to ponder. What would it look like to live in a world where we are no longer threatened by the beliefs of others? What would it be like when we not only accept, but can truly celebrate each other's differences? Would it help to know that the existence of other paths did not violate or lessen the importance or reality of our own? I pondered that perhaps the knowledge that our own fruit exists regardless of how many other fruits are out there might help lessen the fear of being proven wrong.

If people could truly begin to understand what it means that "God is love," then they might no longer fear being led astray. Instead, they could allow their divine curiosity to awaken and to lead them. Instead of fearing the sincere beliefs of others, they would become insatiably curious. Every new understanding and perspective would contribute to their own. We would finally know that God is bigger than the cultural perspective of just one person or just one tradition, and that His love is more embracing than anything we could have imagined. We would hunger for every new revelation as it was provided through the perspective of the experience of each of our brothers and sisters in this world.

Jesus's teaching of how his disciples are to be recognized by their "love one to another" would finally be realized in our capacity to truly listen to each other.[30] There would be no more condescending tones or judgmental attitudes as we talk with people from other religions and beliefs. Each would be embraced. The light of God in each would be celebrated and received as equal to our own. All fruits would be gathered into one great whole as they exist upon the tree of life.

---

[30] "By this shall all men know that ye are my disciples, if ye have love one to another." John 13:35

Part 5

Stillness

Chapter 17

Diving Deeper

After returning home, I began to wonder why the heads of religions, like Swami Nithyananda and other religious leaders, looked so different from their followers. I noticed that their eyes almost always told a story that was not present in others in the religions, a level of enlightenment or communion with the other side that the majority of the followers would likely never obtain. I pondered whether that ultra-enlightened state was less a function of their own diligence and more a state of grace provided because of the responsibility that rested on their shoulders. If so, then what hope did the rest of us have to break through and have true understanding?

This led me to start pondering what it would take for a religion to truly give to its devotees the same fruits as experienced by those at the head. What would it take for each person in a religion to have their eyes opened and experience God to the same degree? When would it be the time of the everyday individual to see, feel, and experience in ways that transformed their way of being and even their physical experience?

It occurred to me that the religions of the past were never designed to lead a man or woman to heaven in this life. They were all about coping with experiences that were beyond our mortal understanding until we reached the other side. It was only the relative few who ever embraced truly divine understanding and experience in this life to the point that their entire beings were changed. It was only the few who "graduated" to a higher state while still in their physical bodies. This filled me with a longing for the day in which the religions of this world would be purified, where they would bestow on their followers the rich gifts that had been described by their founders. And this, not in some experience after this life, but in our present physical state.

It felt to me that the time for the democratization of spiritual fruits was fast arriving in the world. That is, the time when every man, woman, and child would see and share alike in spiritual abundance was coming. This was the day when "the earth shall be full of the knowledge of the Lord, as the waters cover the sea".[31] It was as though I could see the fulfillment of the promise that "they shall not teach every man his neighbour, and every man his brother, saying, Know the Lord: for all shall know (God), from the least to the greatest."[32] My heart was expanding with hope.

Another observation I had after returning from India was that no matter how many times I crossed over, life here seemed largely the same. Every time, I would go from feeling limitless bliss, love, and acceptance, back into the shell of mortal experience with pain, suffering, and fear. While the love would last for a time, it eventually faded. Just like eating, no matter how much I ate, I always needed to eat again.

Rather than experiencing this pattern as an impediment, I saw it and other patterns that presented themselves as opportunities to gain greater insight into the mechanism that prevents us from being continuously aware of the bliss of God's love. I spent large amounts of time in internal observation, like a nature observer full of curiosity witnessing the behavior of the lion free from any judgment. The less I judged, the more it revealed itself to me. The more I observed, the more I understood.

Consequently, this section does not build around a single crossover experience, which reflects a shift in my focus from spiritual visions to more direct and personal integration. Therefore, this section focuses on a series of internal awakenings and understandings that impacted me perhaps more profoundly than my prior crossover experiences as I learned to find truth not just in one place, but in every moment and in every experience. It

---

[31] Isaiah 11:9

[32] Hebrews 8:11

is the truth that sets us free,[33] not the container, or experience, in which the truth is packaged.

Whether the package is a personal experience or even the dogma of countless generations past, at some point we must discern the difference between the package that limits and the truth that liberates. This can be compared to the difference between an artist or musician who flows with an unseen rhythm versus a student who merely reads about art or music. The words can point to what it is like to be a musician, but never make one. At some point, the student must let go of the words and all their definitions of what music "should be" and simply start to hear the inner music. So too is the experience of spiritual truth.

For me, truth increasingly came through internal observation and direct connection with whatever experience I was having. Life was starting to become a more sacred scripture for me than the words recorded in any book or offered even in sacred vision. Crossover experiences have no meaning outside of the truth from which they are made, and truth is the substance of life. Very simply, truth is What Is when we release all our opinions and definitions to constrain it. It is life without a filter. By its very nature the experience of truth liberates us because it does not care about our definitions of self, life, or even God. This is in contrast with the use of "authoritative" sources to limit truth. Rather, truth can be found in every moment and needs no external validation to make it true.

In connection with the need to have crossover experiences, I had a few observations: *Maybe spiritual experiences and spiritual gifts are not the foundation to true happiness and joy in this life. These come and go like so many fleeting thoughts. Then what is the foundation to abiding peace? Perhaps peace itself is more*

---

[33] "And ye shall know the truth, and the truth shall make you free." John 8:32

important than knowledge, bliss, or other experiences. Didn't Jesus say he gave us his peace but not as the world gives?[34]

Something inside me was stirring. *Maybe the purpose of these experiences isn't to perpetuate my human desire to escape from my circumstances. And maybe the experiences themselves are not the answer. Maybe the purpose is to awaken me to a connection with heaven in the body without needing the experiences. But how would I do that?*

My thoughts continued to travel in this direction and were further impacted by my recent immersion in Swami Nithyananda's enlightened presence. *Isn't enlightenment really just the ability to be at peace no matter what is happening around you? Isn't this effectively what Jesus said he was offering, the ability to be at peace no matter what?*

I also pondered how the experience of enlightenment might impact my overall experience of God and heaven, *I wonder if I am supposed to integrate the Christian fruit of seeing the external God with the Hindu fruit of enlightenment? Is this part of what I'm being led to with the idea of multiple fruits? If experiencing God was beautiful by itself, then what would it be like seeing God but also being in a state of unconditional peace? Instead of having just a single fruit from the tree of life, what would a fruit smoothie be like?*

Like many people, my imagination of the experience of enlightenment was probably different than what it really is. After all, how can you imagine something you have never experienced? At that time for me, the idea of enlightenment felt like the release of all stress into a never-ending blissful euphoria. It felt like the end of hardship, not in the physical life, but a feeling of blissful unfolding that continued no matter what the external world was doing. I reasoned that this was what Jesus had experienced when he slept through the storm – he felt the emotion of peace before it

---

[34] "Peace I leave with you, my peace I give unto you: not as the world giveth, give I unto you." John 14:27

manifested in the world around him.[35] I reflected deeply and frequently on the nature of that peace which abides without end.

I also thought often about Swami Nithyananda's words that enlightenment cannot be found by seeking it. This made sense to me at an intuitive level. To seek something means you do not have it. To send out the feeling of "I do not have it" into the light returns the experience of "I do not have it." Therefore, to seek enlightenment is to embark on a quest of endless duration, an ever-receding horizon perpetuated by our very motion. But, how does one go about finding something that can never be found by seeking?

I pondered this question day in and day out. Finally, I arrived at a conclusion – I should use the gift of manifestation within me to create healing and enlightenment. It was just a matter of altering the program, wasn't it? It did not occur to me at the time, that active creation even in spirit is still seeking. Chasing after bliss or any other positive emotion was still a failure to be truly present with life in this moment with all its messiness. So, I dove in, head first into full-time meditation and manifestation of what it would feel like to be fully healed and come to rest.

---

[35] Mark 4:35-41

Chapter 18

Love Attack

Within a few days of beginning to send out that manifestation, a book on my bookshelf jumped out at me, *You Are the Placebo,* by Dr. Joe Dispenza. Someone had given me the book a few years earlier and I simply filed it away in that never-ending supply of books I might someday read.

I pulled it down and opened it. Within the first few paragraphs, I already knew I had to be at his next seminar. Not knowing how quickly his retreats fill up, I looked online and saw a seven-day advanced retreat just two weeks away in Santa Fe, New Mexico. Unfortunately, it was completely full. However, I knew I was supposed to be there and trusted something would show up.

A couple of days later, I again got the feeling I was supposed to be there and checked back online. This time, there was an opening, probably due to a last-minute cancelation. I booked the trip and quickly took his online prerequisites to qualify for the advanced course. And then, I was off to Santa Fe without a day to spare.

Outside of the beautiful meditations and activities, what impacted me the most was that Dr. Joe was the first person I ever met to articulate the principle of creation shown to me in my second experience. He actually put into words the physics of heaven – physics not even I had been able to articulate from my own experience! His understanding of how the principle of manifestation worked contributed to my own. It helped me unlock pieces of my experience I had not understood before, helping me take a leap forward in what heaven had already begun to teach me.

He was especially articulate with the workings of the mind and the process of reprogramming the mind. In one example, he discussed the principles behind a panic attack and then told us it was possible to reprogram the mind to have "love attacks." That is, rather than everything in our environment contributing to anxiety that spirals into crippling negative emotion, everything could remind us of divine love instead. This upward spiral could cause us to lose all control in a swoon of bliss that opened the heavens.

I laughed at the thought, but the very next day, I had the opportunity to experience just such a love attack. During the conference, the blissful forms of kundalini had reopened for me. During one meditation, the bliss was flowing for hours. That afternoon when I sat down for the next part of his lecture, I felt so much joy that the bliss just started flowing without any meditation to trigger it. All I could do was close my eyes and hold on. What was more is that the bliss was triggering more bliss in a way that was exactly opposite to a panic attack.

During Dr. Joe's meditations, there are a lot of people having different experiences. To hear someone cry or make other noises of blissful transformation during the meditation would be considered appropriate because of the setting. However, during his lectures, there is near absolute quiet out of respect for what he is teaching. Suddenly, I found myself in a dilemma. I was starting to have a through-the-veil type experience open up for me and it was the "inappropriate time." I knew if I surrendered to the feeling, my body would likely start quaking with the shifting of consciousness and due to the intensity of the joy I was feeling, I might start audibly expressing myself in a very loud way.

As I observed the emotions rising within me, both those of joy and the inhibitory emotions of social propriety, I understood something. There was a clarity of thought teaching me about the state of heavenly bliss that I wanted to achieve in the physical body. If what I said was true, that is, if I truly wanted to walk in bliss, then I would have to be comfortable doing so around others who were not in that state, just like in this very moment. I was ready to take flight into another realm, but those sitting next to me were starting to pull back. I could feel their thoughts in that spiritual state, *This isn't appropriate right now. Don't draw attention to us. Can't you save that for the meditation?*

While my spirit wanted to expand, they still wanted to be present in this earth realm with all of its rules. I made my choice. I came to this conference for this type of experience and understanding, so I decided to release the inhibitory programs and go head-on into the feeling. My body did indeed start shaking and I was very vocal with the bliss that was flowing through me. I knew those next to me were uncomfortable, but I no longer cared.

Suddenly, I became aware of a shift in the energy and knew that Dr. Joe had singled me out. He came down off the stage and walked out into the audience of nearly one-thousand people to stand right in front of me. The TV cameras were zoomed in on the interaction, and I wondered what was about to transpire. Once again, I felt the temptation to pull back from the experience, but decided that I was having too much fun and wanted to release even deeper.

As I did so, he surprised me with a story of his own. Without interrupting my state, he began telling all those watching the cameras several stories about his own spiritual journeys that took place at socially awkward moments and how those who seek divine love don't always get to choose when it arrives. While I was not expecting him to do this, I was very grateful that he did. It felt like a confirmation of my choice to release in the "inappropriate moment."

That experience of bliss continued to expand with greater intensity for the rest of his lecture and into the meditation that followed. While I did not visit heaven in an out-of-body type experience in that moment, I definitely felt the expansion and was not the least bit concerned that there were no accompanying visuals.

This experience did cause me to think deeply about the limits to having heaven upon earth. To feel heavenly bliss when others are sad or experiencing hardship could feel uncaring. For example, imagine the bliss causing you to spontaneously laugh-out-loud taking place during a funeral. You might be in a state of uninterrupted joy, but social propriety would dictate that you respect the emotional state of others by mirroring what they are feeling. And therein is the problem. Who among us can have heavenly bliss if we are still under the obligation to mirror each other's emotions?

I looked into the depth of the structures that inhibit the bliss and saw layers upon layers of programming that are normally operative. For example, is it appropriate to still feel bliss if you make a mistake? What if others think you made a mistake and expect you to feel bad? At what point is letting go of societal expectations crossing the line to where you become so out of sync with others that you no longer have any impact on this realm?

These questions weren't answered for me in that moment. As so often happened in this phase of learning, the questions were the answers. They were designed to create awareness outside of the structure that had been my unconscious bounds in the past. Awareness created space for change. Change took place outside of time, meaning that it was irrelevant whether the healing of these programs was instantaneous or a little bit at a time. What mattered is that awareness had returned, just like blood flow coming back to an arm or leg that had been asleep. Healing was only a matter of time from there.

Chapter 19

Jumping Off the Telephone Pole

The answer about feeling bliss when you make mistakes came during another activity at the same conference. This was a team building exercise that involved scaling a telephone pole, turning in a circle on top, and then diving off the pole to catch a trapeze a few feet away. The trapeze was supposed to represent our future, and the fear represented our fear of stepping into that future.

The hardest part for me wasn't jumping for the trapeze. By that point, I felt great. What stopped my heart was momentarily having to let go of my relatively safe position on the ladder so that I could put my feet on top of the telephone pole. For all the world, I could not convince my feet to budge. "You can do it!" I faintly heard the shouts from people below. But I really couldn't discern their voices in that moment. Nothing existed except for the wind, which exaggeratedly felt like a hurricane, the top of the pole, and my two left feet. The world teetered all around me. My vision felt like it was swimming as I felt the terror pounding in my chest. I could see the ground nearly forty feet below me.

It was like one of those dreams where you are trying to do something simple but every part of your body feels thick and sluggish. My feet may as well have been two sacks of potatoes, and I knew for a fact that sacks of potatoes would not be stable on the top of that telephone pole.

By this time, I had learned to witness my emotions more so than to be them. While I could feel the adrenaline surge through my entire body, I could also watch the process with a detached interest. *Stepping onto the pole is like getting out of bed in the morning,* I thought. *Why should it be so hard? I literally move my feet in that motion every day. I never once think about it. But here, it is suddenly the most impossible task in the world.*

I could hear the words of Dr. Joe in my mind as well, "How do you know you can't do it? You've never done this before, so it must be your past dictating your future. If you want to create a new future, then you have to break free from your past!"

He was right. I knew I had never been at the top of a telephone pole before. I was even hooked up to a safety harness to prevent me from falling. Why was I so scared? It was fascinating thinking about the emotions that were controlling my physical body and the programming that was subconsciously controlling my emotions.

I stilled my heart beat, going into a meditative state and generated a new emotion, an emotion of success. Before I could think otherwise, I stood up on the telephone pole, turned in a full circle and then leapt off toward the hanging trapeze that symbolized my future.

I felt exhilaration. I had done it! I took a leap of faith, and actually succeeded!

I leaned heavily against the safety harness and let go, being lowered slowly back to the ground. I felt free from my past fears. It was beautiful. But the learning experience was far from over.

With my test behind me, I watched in amusement as others struggled up the ladder to the top of the pole and faced their own inner fears. Some broke down weeping. Others, simply gave up. A few went through the whole process accompanied by the cheers of those below.

But what caught my attention the most was an elderly woman in a wheelchair. It was obvious to everyone she couldn't possibly complete the challenge. But she insisted on being helped out of her chair up to the ladder.

Each of us could see the pain on her face as she challenged her frail bones to do something new. Secretly, we each took up the chant in our hearts wishing for her success. We watched with concern and amazement as she did not let her disability stop her from trying.

She actually succeeded in making it up the first step or two on the ladder before falling off. We all erupted in cheers far louder than we made for even those who completed the challenge. All at once, I understood something. The way we view heaven is backward.

We judge success in the world by whether we complete a task. Those who are at the top of the ladder, metaphorically speaking, are the most praised. Whether in secular or spiritual matters, they are the ones considered the most worthy. And yet, I now understood that in heaven, success is not about completion. It is about trying – often in circumstances we were never meant to overcome. The joy is similar to the roars of approval that come from teenage onlookers after an epic belly-flop. Instead of fingers of derision over what appear to be catastrophic mistakes, there is elation.

This woman was the worst performer out of all of us. And yet, she received the most cheers. She had the most stacked against her. There was no way she could succeed, which was what made her effort all the more valiant. I could see that the only mistakes we make are the experiences we fail to learn from. And for a timeless being, we eventually learn from all experience. Therefore, in the grand scheme of things, there are no mistakes. In fact, if there is anything that might resemble a mistake, it is not failure, it is failing to try. Because the only experience we cannot learn from is the experience we do not have. This is why the rules can be so detrimental at times: they can keep us from even trying. Heaven applauds our biggest belly flops because we had the faith to try even in the midst of what appeared to be certain failure.

This understanding deepened for me in our next meditation after the activity. As part of a manifestation exercise, we were supposed to envision an object and what it would feel like to have that object. I was envisioning always having extra money on hand to give out to random homeless people I encountered. I was moving into the feeling of giving to people in unexpected ways that caused them to feel a sudden state of mercy. In my vision, I would take each one by the shoulders, look into their eyes, and say, "I love you." Immediately, I would embrace them and hold them while we shared a tender moment of humanity together.

But then an interesting thing happened. As I continued to envision giving to the homeless people, eventually I forgot about giving them money and just started hugging them. The money was just an excuse to have a truly human interaction. This was what I really wanted, to share God's love with them by embodying that love. I saw that as I gave them hugs, the love of God came out in such a profound way that I was weeping even just watching it. I would look into their eyes deeply and we would both weep as I said simply, "I love you. You are a divine being. You are cherished."

By this point in the meditation, I had become completely enmeshed in the experience. I was feeling it as though it were happening in real life. To my mind, there was no separation between this experience and reality. In fact, it was starting to take on that element of feeling that is more real than this life. Without the filter of the body, divine emotion is frequently experienced in a much more profound way. I allowed this process to unfold, because I understood how those emotions brought healing to my mind and body in addition to manifesting the synchronicities I knew would follow. What I did not understand as well at the time, is that frequently what we imagine giving to others is what we are deeply craving ourselves. Although I did have some physical experiences with homeless people that showed up after this manifestation, a large portion of this experience was symbolic for me. After my first two crossover experiences, I started trying to structure my life based on what I had seen in heaven. However, I did not understand the symbolism or the timing. Neither did I understand the limitations of our mortal bodies. I created situations that were hard not only for myself, but for many of those that I loved. I felt alienated from my friends, my family, and my religion. I felt completely abandoned and alone – a spiritual beggar with no one left to turn to – a feeling of betrayal by life itself only understood by those who have walked the path of deep discipleship.

As I surrendered to the intensity of the love I was feeling in this exchange, I saw with many tears that some people in this world have never experienced another person looking deeply into their soul and witnessing the truth of their being. I saw that there are people who have never known love before in their entire lives. They have allowed the world around them to dictate their worth and what they believe about themselves. As I observed the flow of divine love in the experience, I understood the potential for complete transformation of life and self-perception simply from someone taking the time to look past everything that is "wrong" and seeing the divine worth within. It is almost like the act of externally witnessing divine character, not through words but through heart-felt connection, is so at odds with the individual's narrative that it causes them to "wake up."

By this point, the meditation was deep enough that it took on a life of its own. I started seeing more and more that I was not creating. This would be like clumsily drawing a stick figure on the chalk board of the mind and then pausing only to see the chalk start moving of its own accord to produce a full-color, three-dimensional masterpiece more beautiful than anything you could have ever imagined. Instantly, the scene changed. I was no longer on the street. Instead, I was in heaven standing in front of God and He was looking into my eyes. All of the feelings I have had on previous occasions with God came flooding in like a tidal wave, overwhelming me with love that brought me to my knees in tears. The intensity of the feeling was such that I could not for all the world look away or see anything outside of His person enveloped in light, but I still felt my being wanting to twist away from those eyes. It was not my eyes that tried to flee, but my heart that could not take the absolute love and acceptance with which He embraced me. Despite having had this type of experience in the past, I was no more prepared for how beautiful this experience was or how the love almost hurt. It was like the very first time all over again, except this time I did not feel worthy of his love. Notwithstanding the feeling of wanting to shrink, I felt Him raising my spiritually lowered face, as though His very essence were the hand enveloping my heart, until I could look Him fully in the eyes. He then proceeded to take me by the shoulders just as tenderly as I had imagined doing with the homeless people and said with feeling and meaning far greater than any I had imagined, "I love you."

Those words were like life itself. I cannot convey what power, emotion, and meaning were embodied in such a simple phrase. It was like the entire essence of my being and the true nature of God were contained within them. On top of that, He was using the understanding I had just gained in my manifestation to teach me a principle. Even as my deepest desire had been to look into the eyes of the individuals that society had cast out to find a divine beauty worthy of worship, so now was He looking past everything that I had condemned myself over. This especially included those choices that caused me so much pain and deep reflection. I felt I could not forgive myself for trying to take a leap into the spiritual realm and falling so short of what I thought to accomplish. But, He did not see what others believed were my faults; only the divine light that I was blind to. All my foibles and missteps were sacred because they had been teachers of a divine being in embryo. Mistakes, even what appear to us to be our biggest and most unforgivable mistakes, were not to be feared or fretted over, because they are our teachers just as much as our successes are.

The feeling of this experience was in complete contrast with my first crossover experience where I was being interviewed by the messengers. During that interview, I felt worthiness and joy in part because of my perceived obedience and conformance to the religious pattern I had been taught. Here, I entered the experience feeling I had failed. This brought an entirely new kind of joy and a completely different perspective on the feeling of mercy, love, and absolute acceptance. I knew what it was to be without judgment all the more by virtue of having felt so much self-judgment only moments before. It was the experience of God lifting my face from the depths to see the perfection in all that was, to see how the perfection was all the greater by virtue of what the world called "mistakes." It was the joy of redemption, of feeling loved inside my experience. In both instances, there was joy. God accepted me in ways I could not comprehend in each. But in this latter instance, the feeling in my heart was all the more expansive by virtue of the contrast.

The layers of meaning and symbolism in the way he embraced me exactly how I imagined embracing the homeless connected all at once, allowing His love to enter my heart with the force of a freight train. I lost all emotional control at this point. I was weeping openly in both the vision and my physical body. Referring to the desire in my heart to take care of the outcasts, the words of Jesus came to mind, "…inasmuch as ye have done it unto one of the least of these my brethren, ye have done it unto me."[36] As we release the judgment we carry for others, we are actually just releasing the infinite burden of self-judgment. As we open our hearts to those who have no place in society, we open our hearts to the outcast parts of ourselves. This is why we are told to love without limit. This lesson was driven home all the more because I felt like an outcast in my home, my religion, and the world around me. But God did not see those things; He saw that which was beautiful in me even if no other person could. I was not alone. In my vision, I desired to give to all of these beggars; now I was the beggar. I was loved and accepted by God in ways I could not imagine. Here, He was looking into my eyes with my soul on fire from the love I was experiencing.

My weeping continued uncontrollably. All the hurt I had been feeling just came up and was swept away. I felt intense vibrations all over my being. Even after the meditation was formally over, I could not stop the experience from continuing to unfold. I went out into the hall and found a quiet space to continue the meditation for another hour or so. What I saw continued to expand. The vibration within me increased. The bliss increased until the vision from my second crossover experience a few years earlier returned to me. Only now I saw it with new eyes. I saw the limited perspectives from which I had interpreted those experiences, and I saw the perfection arising from my misunderstandings.

I understood that these misunderstandings were not just limited to my own experiences. They exist in every spiritual path

---

[36] Matthew 25:40

185

around the world. It is human nature to understand what we are shown and/or taught through the limited experience we have. How could we do anything other than misunderstand heavenly love? In fact, I saw this misunderstanding as being a huge part of our purpose here on earth. There was nowhere else where we could be sufficiently blinded to our own nature to make mistakes. In this way, both our mistakes and the mistakes of others were holy and sacred gifts from God. While we suffered from them here, I saw that they were transformed in the most beautiful way possible on the other side. It was like there was a divine seed which was the true essence of our every experience that only needed exposure to divine love to sprout. When the near-infinite divine seeds in our experiences sprouted, then heaven erupted in all its glory. This joy was all the greater from the contrast between the intensity of societal and self-judgment here and God's absolute acceptance there.

Not only that, but I also saw that those who release judgment in exchange for the love of God in this life could begin that transformation in the here and now without having to wait. Self-judgment was only an inhibitor to the joy that each of us came to create. By becoming aware of the layers on which we store it and then releasing it, we could truly begin the experience of heaven on earth. As I began to see more fully how our misunderstandings in this life have the potential to be converted to such joy, I could finally start to appreciate the joy heaven has when we have the faith to jump without having even a prayer of success.

Chapter 20

Unity

The next morning was cold, frigid even. It was twenty years to the day from when I had been baptized by water and the Spirit. We were awake at an obscenely early hour of the morning to stand in the winter chill of the low-lying Santa Fe mountains. Nearly a thousand people stood outside of the hotel where the retreat was being held. We were waiting for the instruction to start our walking meditation.

A walking meditation is a bridge between the inner silence sometimes achieved in deep meditation and waking life. It brings the intention to access the temple of silence and powerful creation discovered in those moments even while moving about our daily lives. At that moment, however, I was doing my best to stay positive about the experience. My teeth were chattering uncontrollably. As I waited for the official start, I mulled over the ideas that resulted in my attendance at the conference.

I wanted to focus my manifestations into a better way for the earth to transition. Could I see the world rising and transforming through awakening in bliss rather than through burning in pain? For me, this was more than figurative; the connection between personal awakening in unfolding layers of bliss and the awakening of the world as a whole was all too real. It was impossible to release the inhibitions to the presence of God in one without sending powerful ripples through the other. That was exactly what I had understood from my second crossover experience.

Thus, the idea of a blissful transformation of the earth was very much present in my heart. And it was very much connected with the idea of personal ascension. These thoughts were deeply imprinted upon my soul: *Do you want to help the world? Then wake up – and go deeply into god consciousness experiencing a fullness of joy in your mortal body. This is the most important thing that you can do.*

I had evidence of this idea in my own home. Frequently, aspects of my relationship with my children that I had struggled with for years would spontaneously change following a meditation where I experienced deep, healing insight into my own nature. Over and over again, I saw the effect at a personal level where the relationship changed spontaneously in ways that years of effort could not touch. It was a logical extension that the same principle would apply to society on a larger scale. It was simply a matter of experiencing the code on a deeper level in the Light. In my heart, I knew I was not alone in this practice either. There were many others in cultures from around the world having similar realizations. Without seeing each other, somehow we were each acting as one, contributing to the transformation of the earth and what it means to be human. The awakening happening in one was happening in all. The increase in light before dawn may be faint at first, but it increases the clarity in the world for all, including those who are not yet awake to see it.

This particular morning as we did our walking meditation, I began to envision being filled with the bliss of full awakening. This led me to another thought – despite my conscious manifestation of allowing the light of God to walk unrestricted in the flesh, I still saw myself as separate from that light. I felt a fear and resistance to the idea that the light within each of us might actually be the light of God. In fact, it might have been the most terrifying thought in the world to me at that time – that somehow the consciousness within us from which we arise and have our being *is* God.

While I had released many of my fears in prior experiences, yet like many others in this world, I still had opportunities to revisit them for greater understanding and growth. Perhaps this fear was so persistent because it had some of its roots in Western understanding of God, that humankind is lower than the dust. Or perhaps it had its roots in the idea of a physical God. It seemed that I could either believe that God had a body like ours, or that God was Light, but to believe both was not permissible. Yet, the irony is that each of us have bodies and we are also Light, so why do we withhold that possibility from God? Moreover, whether

He had a body or was only Light really wasn't the point. In either event, I conceived of God as separate from my existence. In fact, I needed God to be separate from my existence in order to maintain coherence in my worldview. To my limited understanding, the overwhelming hardships of life could only make sense if there were a God separate from my being. To believe oneself equal with God was the ultimate temptation; to the extent that I still believed in sin, this was the ultimate sin. Not because God would not forgive it, but because in buying into this idea, we would no longer be teachable. I also had fears stemming from the time before I was baptized. It was in connection with this belief of being one with God that I encountered the dark and the fear. However, as is so often the case, I was not aware of the inconsistencies in the fear, only its presence.

As I saw the fear, I could hear many of the conversations I had with God in the past. I realized He had been leading me inexorably toward this conclusion for quite some time. Why was I still resisting it? Why was I afraid of it? If He was trying to reveal it to me, shouldn't I embrace it? I had been feeling God tell me to let go of clinging to Him in an external way and trust the light within me. It was the sensation that He wanted me to let go of hanging on to Him so tightly so that I could finally see the reflection. He wanted me to see what he had been trying to show me all along – the god in me.

It was not enough for me to worship Him for all eternity in an external way. This would amount to salvation without understanding, which is not really salvation at all. This would not satisfy His purposes for me. He wanted me and each of His children to evolve to understand the truths that make Him God and to see that those truths are also in each of us, not in some distant heaven, but in the present moment. All we lack is awareness, like the effect of rain on seeds after a long winter, for them to be activated. A full awakening meant to receive all that the Father has.[37] What the Father has is more than the physical substance of this universe. At its center is the matrix of salvation, a full experience of joy as it exists in the heart of God. It means to see as He sees, to know as He knows, to understand as He understands – the fullness of the glory of God in the physical body. Like a truly loving father, this was His greatest joy, to help that same joy awaken within us by becoming like Him. However, this concept went beyond intellectual understanding. Whether He was Light, a body, or both, the true nature of existence could not awaken within me as long as I continued to avoid deep understanding.

While I understood these things in an intellectual way, it was obvious by the fear still in my heart that these realities had not penetrated into the deepest levels of my being. Finally, I told Him, "I surrender. If you really want to reveal this to me, then I let go and allow." I did not understand it at the time, but this was the answer to my earlier questions about how to receive something that cannot be found through seeking. It is also the pattern behind each of my experiences. It was not the seeking that brought them; rather they came in the moment I finally let go and surrendered, when the grace within my heart was simply allowed. This is the moment when the deepest joys within are no longer contained or constrained, but allowed to bubble over in their own time and their own way. It is the moment when we stop defining God and let Him define us. It is the moment when we cease to tell our hearts what we should want or that we are unworthy. Instead, we allow the light as it exists in the purity of our hearts to manifest through us, as us. This is the secret to bringing real change into the world: let go of the idea that the ego which manifested the problems to begin with can ever solve them from within its limited perception. Stop trying to control or constrain the outcome. You cannot change the illusion by fighting with the illusion. Instead, allow the solutions from a more Loving

---

[37] "The Spirit itself beareth witness with our spirit, that we are the children of God: And if children, then heirs; heirs of God, and joint-heirs with Christ" Romans 8:16-17

Intelligence to manifest through us. Yield our bodies to the creations of a Higher Love.

There are many teachers out there sharing parts of these principles, especially with respect to manifesting a better future for ourselves and others. I want to take this principle a step further. While we can individually manifest cars, houses, relationships, etc, at some point our souls desire something more. When the expression of the physical world is seen to no longer impact our true happiness, there is a desire to move through the wall that separates us from God. There is a desire to comprehend the nature of existence itself. This happens in a more feminine way, that is not through force or exertion, but by allowing the joy that comprises our hearts and all things to bubble over into this world. It is to yield the manifestation to a Greater Love.

I shivered against the cold again and returned my attention back to the meditation. I allowed Spirit inside me to lead me in the visualization. That is, I let go of my resistance and allowed the inner emotions originating from outside my conscious awareness to take over the manifestation. I saw myself coming into a fullness of the realization of my unity with the divine being. I saw my walls coming down to receiving this revelation. I saw God manifesting it in me in such a way that I finally understood. I felt the joy I would have in being able to walk as a living expression of the love of God upon the earth. As with other manifestations, I did not just see these things; I experienced them, allowing the flow of new emotions to heal deep hurts that I did not know were there. In short, I got out of the way of my enlightenment and allowed God to manifest it through me.

Then finally, I stopped for the final part of the meditation and watched the sun rise. No matter how much I have tried to release into the light within me in the past, there has always been a hurdle. Something has always held me back. There has been a conflict, but this time, I understood what God has been trying to show me from the beginning. As the sun came up, I finally saw. When I say "saw" in this instance it is different from how I have used the term before. In all of my crossover experiences, there was a spiritual energy which was sufficiently powerful as to create visual experience within me. In this instance, seeing was not related to the intensity of the energetic and emotional experience. Rather, it was simple awareness.

There was light, or consciousness. Consciousness was the light of awareness. Everything around me in my perceived experience had its existence within consciousness. It was all light. It all enveloped me. The part of consciousness I perceived as "me" was similar to an infant perfectly enveloped in the womb of my Mother's love. All of consciousness formed that living womb. This included everything from my physical body and the world around me to my thoughts, emotions, and perceptions of that world. The entire experience had its being in the most intimate form of the love of God, all of which was there for my learning and joy.

I saw that while I once perceived the womb of the external world as separate from myself, it in fact arises from consciousness the same as I do. Somehow, I was both the infant and the womb. It truly was like seeing the tail of the dog that is happily wagging to see you, only to find that it is your own. All of creation was loving and happy to see me precisely because I was part of it – not separate from it. It was God embracing God in a union more intimate than any lover could ever give. Only, the body of my awareness was still growing. Hence, I was created in the image of God but was still a child in potential realization of unity with the light; I was a child of God nestled in the bosom of creation. Just like Jesus when he walked the earth, each of us is a fullness of the light in a growing body of awareness. We may have different roles than what he came to do, but we have the same potential for infinite realization. Waking up to that potential and experiencing it unfolding within us is a big part of the salvation he came to bring.

I saw that my body grows in measure with its capacity to connect awareness with the fullness of light, releasing lower vibration patterns in consciousness. This liberation of energy through growing understanding and awareness is experienced as joy. The experience of joy in this process is a scaled-down version of the self-perpetuating release of energies that causes God's body to glow brilliantly in the joy of eternal release. Like the never-changing-to-us process of nuclear fusion in the sun, the joy of eternal release catalyzes even greater release. I saw that this process was going on inside me even before becoming aware of it. In fact, it is going on inside of all of us, lacking only our individual awareness to see the joy that has always been there.

In that moment, I could feel the dual nature of it all. I could see the way my body perceived the experiences in that womb as separate and yet, simultaneously see the light of consciousness that was its true identity. There was both separation and unity, a dual reality. Only, unity was found not in the distinction between these two states, but in the confluence between them. In that moment, I felt no need to define those states or to quantify my experience. Awareness was expanded beyond the limitations of that self which needs comparison to validate its existence. There was only understanding.

Awareness did not preclude the existence of a physical God any more than turning on a light in a room obviates the existence of those within it. I could still feel the presence of the physical being of God in my awareness, and yet, like the rest of the physical world, could also feel the unity underlying all awareness. At this time, the emphasis was simply shifted from the physical form of God as separate from me to the light of consciousness which made up my experience of the physical God. He was just as real as the rocks or the trees around me, but even as each of these were comprised of consciousness, so too was He. My awareness was centered on this experience of consciousness from which all things arise and have their being. It existed underneath my conceptions of self, similar to the foundation which exists beneath a house. Only, rather than being underneath in a separate way like a house foundation would be, it was more like the quantum energy from which physical form arises – the wave behind the particle that is the true nature of the particle itself.

I saw that this light was more me than any of my limited understandings or conceptions of self. Yet, in that inexplicable way that has tongue-tied those returning from near-death experiences, it was also God. God could never judge me because He could never judge Himself. This understanding caused me to laugh as though I were sharing the greatest joke of creation with God. In a moment, so much stress that I carried came out with that laughter. My mirth was in the irony behind my fear of displeasing God. That fear was like the shadow worrying about displeasing the body that casts it. I was the shadow and God was the body. Yet, my awareness until then had been unable to see the unity between the two.

It was like the feeling of seeing and recognizing an old friend after years of separation, only better. The old friend was the intimate portion of me. It was the real me. However, in some divine irony, I was also the limited being who was witnessing this process. I laughed with the understanding that the reason God could never judge this limited being I conceived of as me was that we were one. In the light of awareness, I would never judge myself. He was more intimate with me than a lover could ever be. We shared consciousness. There was no separation. There was only What Is.

It was nothing like I had previously imagined it, but it did not need to be either. I had built up an almost cult-like devotion to the idea of enlightenment, not understanding that this romanticization was no more real than a teenager's idea of love. Instead of all that I had imagined, there was understanding. There were no lights. No bells. No whistles. The flowery language used to describe it seems to lead away from it rather than to it. It was as simple as the sun rising in front of me. It just was. I could see what had always been plainly in front of me, not because there was an increase in light, but because the light of my awareness had become truly present. The light had always been there, I simply had never come to rest long enough to be aware of it.

There was no measuring up to my own or anyone else's standard of what that experience should look like. The light did not ebb or flow with my conception of worthiness. It was always there. I was always loved and enveloped perfectly, not by an external influence, but by something that was as much me as the body and beliefs I had come to associate with.

The expanse of awareness might be compared to the difference between how you see your lawn and how a botanist might see it. Most days, you probably only notice there is grass. If you look a little bit closer, you may realize that the grass is full of tiny weeds. For some homeowners, they may fight with these weeds year in and year out. For the botanist, awareness has deepened, allowing them to see in these weeds multitudes of tiny flowers from diverse species that support the local wildlife. They see the importance of the smallest plant in maintaining the diversity of life. Rather than a nuisance, they are a miracle. Under the lens of the microscope, those small flowers open up a whole new and breathtaking world that only a small number are ever initiated into. What were once weeds, suddenly through awareness, are transmuted into one of life's most sublime joys. It is impossible to be grateful for that which we are unaware and for that which we have no understanding.

Despite the enlightened perspective on the beauty of life, it does not mean the botanist's yard is devoid of weeds. In fact, in their joy of learning they may even encourage a few more weeds in their yard, much to the dismay of their neighbors. Instead of achieving a perfectly manicured lawn, their relationship to the weeds has changed. They can now see them with a joy and understanding that was not previously available. A weed is no longer defined as the unwanted plants in society but rather the limitations in human understanding that keep people from seeing the beauty in all life. So too is expanded awareness.

Likewise, the climatologist who studies the weather may know the roots of weather patterns. They may be aware of subtle differences in temperature and air pressure that the rest of the world is largely ignorant of. And yet, their awareness does not prevent the rain clouds. They still have just as many rainy days. However, they are no longer in opposition with the weather, but in a state of deep fascination for its beauty and power. So too is expanded awareness.

There was no removal of the weeds in my garden or the clouds in my skies as I once might have imagined. I was not clothed in bliss or heavenly vision. I simply understood the roots to patterns in consciousness that had not been previously available to me. Like the botanist, I suddenly found appreciation for these tiny flowers that once had vexed me. As my awareness of the true nature of these tiny plants in consciousness increased, so too did my gratitude. Not only is it impossible to be grateful for what we do not understand, it is impossible to understand that which we fear. For once, my fear of life was removed, and I stood naked in my awareness of connection to all of life.

I spent half my life suicidal and depressed. I never wanted to be here, but to return back "home," that is to return to the other side. Enlightenment and related experiences are not about escaping this world through bliss, but about accepting this space in all its pain and messiness. It is about being truly present in the journey. It is the choice to make this life "home," to make this life heaven on earth. Heaven is found through acceptance of What Is, not through painfully or fearfully trying to force change on the divine wisdom we have yet to recognize.

If anything, the capacity to truly love others and accept them as they are increased with this experience. I came to understand that as much as we try to love others, we cannot do so as long as we feel separate from God. The possibility that God (and this extends to all the voices of authority in our lives, including and especially our families) might be disappointed in us invokes a sense of judgment for self – if we were to ever cross the unspoken boundaries. We may try to love others who cross these boundaries, but the latent judgment within self can still be felt by them. The presence of this latent judgment of self will be picked up by others as judgment of their thoughts and life choices – even if you are trying to love them. This is why attempts by conservative religions to love others are often felt as judgment instead of love. Thus, the energy of self-judgment prevents the flow of love as it exists in the presence of God.

Even if you feel no judgment for yourself in this moment, the seeds of self-judgment are there waiting to be activated the moment life leads you on an unexpected path. In other words, even dormant seeds of judgment still inhibit the experience and flow of divine love to all the expressions of life in this moment. When your acceptance of self is conditional, so too is your love of others. In other words, the fruit of loving and healing others unconditionally cannot grow from seeds where self is only accepted conditionally. Healing of self must be done in order to love as God loves. This is a nearly-opposite conception of love from what many religions teach: love that is without conditions and not because of conditions.

In this arising awareness, there was no sense of ego, of "I am something that others are not." In fact, it was just the opposite – there was true humility in the awareness that there is no one other than What Is. That is, each of us have the same degree of connection and divine privilege as any other. The herald angels who announced the birth of Christ, may as well have sounded at the birth of each and every child. For in every child is the seed of awakening to realize a fullness of divine experience. They may not have the same role of awakening others in this life that Jesus had, but they are every bit as much sons and daughters of God as Jesus. Each of us is as lovingly embraced in awakening within the bosom of God as an only child, as though all experience were orchestrated purely for our benefit. Have you ever wondered what the infinite intensity of love and joy in God's heart is manifesting? It is you in this exact moment, exactly as you are, with all of your imperfections. In this way, Jesus's title, "Only-Begotten," honors his role as a living revelation of how we are each begotten. We are literally created in the image of God. We have only to awaken to see the perfection in what appears to be imperfection.

My understanding of Jesus's words changed entirely. No more were they rigid words to qualify for a future heaven. Rather, they were words of awakening designed to sprout when the world was ready to rise. And I heard his voice not only in Biblical scripture but in every religion and in every person and in every molecule on the face of the earth. In all of them breathed the life and light, in all of them was the perfect awareness of What

Is. They were all my teachers, and they were all my students. Though one, yet we learned and grew from the experience of many.

Chapter 21

Integrating the Colors of Heaven: Collective and Community Enlightenment

No longer are we to grow on the wings of just one person. For too long, the world has asked the spiritual giants to carry the weight – to literally and metaphorically ascend the mountain and know God so they don't have to.[38] Never in the world's history has this succeeded in bringing heaven to earth, rather only in creating the myth that spirituality is found in separating from the earth. For the first time, we have the chance to try something truly bold, a new experiment: an experiment where we awaken together. This awakening is not built around the visions of just one person or culture, but comes from the space that is created as multiple individuals who have each entered through their respective gate come together as one. Like a flock of birds or school of fish moving as one, it is the enlightenment of the whole and not just an individual. It is an awakening that is benefitted and accelerated all the more by virtue of our collective diversity.

In our masculine world, businesses and even religions have been built like the story in the Dr. Seuss book, *Yertle the Turtle.* In it, the king of all the turtles is made greater by standing on the backs of other turtles so that he can see more, and consequently rule more. The CEO who earns the most generally does so by standing on the shoulders of more people. I wonder how much religious and spiritual leaders do the same, receiving a larger spiritual salary (e.g. in terms of awakening or spiritual gifts) than what the rest of those in the religion receive? While this model has worked well for our world in the past, I wonder what might happen if a new model were implemented in business and

---

[38] "And all the people saw the thunderings, and the lightnings, and the noise of the trumpet, and the mountain smoking: and when the people saw it, they removed, and stood afar off. And they said unto Moses, Speak thou with us, and we will hear: but let not God speak with us, lest we die." Exodus 20:18-19

religion alike where the fruits are democratized for all to receive together? Rather than a single person or group of people at the top receiving all the benefit, arms are linked in a circle. There is no one person more important or elevated than the rest. All grow together.

Collectively pulled by the heart of God, individually we act. All across the face of the earth from a variety of different cultures we feel the call. Even while unaware of each other, we act as one. It is unavoidable. Something inside us pulls and draws us to go ever deeper into an understanding of the divine that takes us beyond the cultural limitations and perspectives of our past. It is no longer enough to live a "good" life the way our respective cultures have defined it. The heart of God calls us to open the veil and partake of comprehension in the flesh.

Comprehending and releasing the veil means that we may come face to face with the fears that have bound our respective cultures and ancestors, the very walls that shut them down. There may be points in time where we have to walk against the flow of tradition and expectation. This process may pull and tug at our innermost heart strings from time to time. However, if we can see beyond the wall, then we can comprehend the joy of what is taking place.

I understand deeply what it feels like to come face-to-face with truths that disrupt the foundation of understanding that we have built our lives upon. For me, many of these were truths I did not ask for, but that came into my mind, heart, and understanding in a way that I could no longer deny. Yes, it is true I was seeking for deeper understanding of the principles I believed with all my heart, but never at any time did it enter into my mind that what I would see might disrupt the tender way that I and those around me viewed the world. I have felt intimately and personally the rejection from friends, family, and loved ones whose religious understanding and societal upbringing prevented them from seeing the truths blossoming within my heart. It hurt that despite having seen and known my character over the course of many years, their inner judgments prevented them from taking the time to truly listen to the awakening understanding that was so beautiful to me. The inexpressible joy of my liberation was instead greeted with judgment and misunderstanding – the blossoming of my peace was their blasphemy. Even where others sincerely tried to listen, I still felt misunderstood and unseen. For all my description of what I was experiencing, I found that others were generally unable to see beyond the walls of their own worldview, the boundaries of the cocoon that incubates them. More importantly, I felt the heartbreak that came from disappointing my younger self who shared a belief in all those same structures with unquestioning devotion.

The straight and narrow path that Jesus spoke of is not the traditions and teachings of any one religion, but the process required of those from all spiritual paths to yield what they believe is true to a Greater Love such that our hearts are changed.[39] It is a deeper discipleship, a dedication to the inner light, that is proven out through willingness to walk completely alone. It is the process of continuously releasing hold of what we think we know in exchange for that moment-to-moment connection with the divine in the center of our beings. No one else can tell us what that path is; it must be discerned from within our own being. We must ultimately answer to the truth in our own hearts no matter how loudly the voices in the world around us protest. This is the cost of breaking forth from our personal cocoon of spiritual incubation: to discern the difference between the truth in our hearts that is part of the awakening butterfly and the voices that still form the remaining fibers of our cocoon.

Although there are moments where we may feel intensely alone, the evolution of consciousness on a personal and global scale was never truly meant to be done on our own. Even at the start of the journey, we were aided by others. Family members, spiritual traditions, and the voices of others helped create the

---

[39] "Enter ye in at the strait gate: for wide is the gate, and broad is the way, that leadeth to destruction, and many there be which go in thereat: Because strait is the gate, and narrow is the way, which leadeth unto life, and few there be that find it." Matthew 7:13-14

walls of our future cocoon through projection of their boundaries and self-judgments upon us. We left the self-oriented teenage mindset and entered the cocoon to undergo our spiritual transformation by accepting those fears and judgments as our own. These fears and judgments helped protect the fragile state of consciousness we found ourselves in at the time as we learned to love and respect each other within the illusion. However, as the butterfly within (i.e. consciousness) begins to wake up from the illusion, an understanding arises that while the cocoon of fears and judgments protected us, it also perpetuated the very veil we sought to overcome in order to commune with heaven. The fears, judgments, and assumptions of reality stemming from society and our ancestors do not exist in the full glory of the love of God and are the fabric of the veil that appears to separate us from the divine.

Here again, we were never meant to do it alone. While at first, the judgments of others formed walls of protection in our transformation, in this stage of our evolution the voices of others and their self-judgments projected upon us form the opposition necessary to strengthen our wings and prepare us to fly. What once were loving boundaries are now the resistance we need to grow. It is not that we hate the resistance or even struggle against the now encroaching boundaries of the cocoon. We must recognize even in the appearance of restriction the love that encapsulates us for our growth and evolution. Learning to relax our hearts and receiving the chaffing of the cocoon as love is still the most effective way to grow. Entering into resistance of any form shuts down our growth and prevents the natural birth of the butterfly from taking place.

We seem to be alone during this phase precisely because the strength to fly depends on the personal discernment developed while differentiating our inner truth from the voices forming the cocoon. It is part of the process of learning to love the butterfly more than the cocoon. The boundaries that formed the walls of our identity while in the cocoon were not us, but just the scaffolding that held space while we discovered what truly was us. The butterfly we are becoming is a sovereign being who understands and lives its own joy in the brightness of God's love. A butterfly who is freed from its cocoon without the struggle of developing discernment will invariably fail to thrive because it does not have the wing strength to survive outside of the relative safety of the cocoon. However, we can still support each other even in this phase through authentic witnessing of each other's journeys, from the courage received in seeing the examples of others going through similar stages of healing and evolution. The path of strengthening our wings by our willingness to walk alone in our inner truth is the path that each of us must ultimately take in order to come forth into spiritual freedom and community with those of like mind. It is the straight and narrow path that those from all backgrounds must ultimately take if they are to awaken in this life.

Supporting each other in this evolution does not mean that we push others to see what we see or to understand what we understand on a personal or a societal level. We may think we are helping a caterpillar in its evolution by pushing it along, when in fact we are damning a species of butterfly with a different timing of evolution than our own. It is not for us to force or determine the timing of the various stages of spiritual evolution, including in ourselves, but to take joy in a Loving Intelligence which is greater than our own that is operative in all life. Trust and surrender in the timing of this Loving Intelligence in a way that unshackles the emotions of our own heart will do more for the healing and transformation of our loved ones and society around us than most any other action. This is because the blossoming of the flower is more affected by the emergence of the sun's light and warmth than by all the howling of the wind. As we release the clutter in our hearts by coming to feel the perfection of imperfection in this moment, we make space for the light to shine through us in a way that helps all the dormant seeds in those around us begin to sprout as well. They will sprout in a timing that benefits our own awakening and theirs, in the most joyous circumstance and time.

The fully-emerged butterfly is also benefitted by community. It is precisely when the butterfly emerges that it is able to congregate with the myriad other species of butterflies floating through the heavens. The ongoing evolution to raise the earth is a collective effort resulting from coming together, each in our respective traditions. It is a joyful reunion of the various types of butterflies, each formed with their own purpose.

Like every other butterfly, this path has cost me everything – the whole cocoon. Yet, there is nothing I would withhold; the price for me has been worth it, even beyond worth it. The breaking of the egg is not painful when we come from the perspective of the baby chick that is emerging into light. We need not fear the changes in the world and our society as they come. We can stand in a space of peace and connection to the light in all things as the world around us, both on a personal and eventually a global level, is reorganized and reorchestrated for our benefit.

Some of us have also received the call to look beyond borders and boundaries that have divided us. We hear the voice asking for unity. Our hearts, without us even knowing it, send out the joyful cry into the light. It is a plea for unity, for that connection we knew before this life, for a love which exceeds cultural and religious boundaries. It is a cry for respect, for dignity, to learn from each and every one of God's children, to value even the most underprivileged of souls.

My question for you is what does your heart say? What is the voice within you asking? What have you heard while you have read and pondered the words in this book? How is it moving you? Perhaps it would be worthwhile taking a few quiet moments to ponder and reflect, to envision how your life might be different. Even better, take a moment to write out what you have felt. If there truly were no bounds, if anything in your heart could be brought forth, what is truly and deeply underneath it all? I'm talking about more than just the material items and relationships: what would you create if you could walk as the full and pure expression of divine joy on this earth, if your heart was truly unbounded?

We may feel alone at times, but there are more of us than you might imagine. Each of us are unique expressions of that divine love, precisely calculated for liberation of patterns of consciousness within our cultures and ancestry. Despite our differences, there is a commonality – that yearning to feel, to grow, to understand, to connect. Each of our expressions is important. We are all necessary to the whole. Even a small handful of us penetrating the illusion that separates us from the divine sends ripples throughout the whole, changing the possibilities of what will be. And there are far more than a small handful of us. There are too many now to stop what has started.

Wherever you are, reflect deeply on your contribution. Reflect on your path. Are you where the joy of your heart leads you to be? Are you making the choices today you came here to make? Do you have the courage to leap? Do you have the trust to fail and still be lovingly held? Can you relax the patterns within you that have bound you and your ancestors? If you were truly at rest, unconditionally loved without a need to do anything, what would you do differently?

This is a time when we get to experience the divine as more than just a physical being separate from us. While the experience of the physical God is beautiful, we are also invited to know Him/Her/Them as the substance that makes up all things, to comprehend life and even God. It is within you and all around you. It is the structure of divine joy from which we arise and have our conscious being. It is in this comprehension of the structure of all life that the veil shall be rent for all. We have that chance to participate, to be a part of the rending of the veil and the coming forth of light that shall lift people in all their respective paths and traditions.

It is not necessary for everyone in this life to master all the other gates. The function of the various spiritual paths are like the parts of the elephant. Some are needed to be the leg, others the tail, and so on. Each part simply needs to stop resisting the others and offer its joy to those who want to receive it. It is as each part works in harmony with the others that the whole is benefitted. Coming through the gate simply changes the perspective from being separate from the elephant leg to *being* the elephant leg.

The reason we come together anyway, even when we are not called to go through others' gates, is that there is greater joy when there is coherence between the inner and outer creation. When the inner world supports the outer world, there is joy, and visa-versa. That is, the outer reflection of all life supporting the growth of the whole is in congruence with the inner state of feeling all things lifting joyfully together. It is in the synergy of the different fruits within the various gates that growth reaches its most joyous and successful state.

For me, this is like assembling the parts of a car. Experiential Buddhism (as opposed to doctrinal teachings) is like the clutch of the car. In experiencing the release of all narrative, the clutch is pressed in, allowing the vehicle to shift gears. Hinduism is like the gas pedal where dissolution into causeless bliss provides unending power to move the vehicle. New Age teachings on manifesting are like the steering wheel, giving us power to direct our journey. Christian understandings of a loving God remind me of the GPS, which directs our vehicle with a Loving Intelligence beyond our own. Other cultures and teachings provide more functionality to the car. The vehicle is unable to function to its fullest potential until it has been completely assembled. Thus, our greatest growth is in the reintegration of truths that were never meant to be separated to begin with.

This is a lot like my career. It was only in merging the disciplines of DNA science, mathematical modeling, international entrepreneurship, intellectual property law, marketing, and others that I was able to not only invent never-before-seen technology but see it distributed to millions around the world. The academic disciplines by themselves were insufficient to accomplish the change in the world my heart so greatly desired to see. They needed to be integrated to unlock their true power.

This is also like the theory of evolution. For years, scientists conjectured that evolution occurred through the accumulated learning of a species via single-base changes in the structure of its DNA over time. However, the fossil data preserved in the earth showed that there were explosions in the number of life forms that happened too fast to come from single-base mutations. Rather, the data then pointed to a new idea: species evolved individually for a time and then *shared* the programming stored in their DNA, allowing for the exponential growth in the number of life forms seen across the planet. Likewise, it is the sharing of well-preserved information in our respective cultures that allows us to take exponential steps in spiritual evolution. This can only happen as we stop looking to the religious and spiritual teachings of others to confirm our own beliefs, and instead start truly listening to what is unique in each other's experiences.

So, which religion/spiritual path is true? Over the last several years I read hundreds of near-death experiences where individuals experienced God. After my own experiences, I realized that heaven was not at all like what I originally imagined. Where once I was closed in my understanding and only wanted to read those experiences that confirmed my beliefs, I became hungry to see what I was still missing. As I read the experiences of others, I found it fascinating that God never once tells someone that they are getting it wrong. It doesn't matter which culture, religion, political persuasion, or lifestyle they come from, each is perfectly accepted and loved *exactly* as they are.

In the few cases where someone actually asks God which religion is right, the answer is always one of two answers: either, "They're all true," or, "None of them are." Can you see how these answers are the same? In a way, asking which religion is true is the wrong question. It's like asking which part of the car is true – the steering wheel, the gas pedal, etc? Or like asking which subject in the university is true? A better question is which one do you feel joy in being a part of? Which one causes your inner being to blossom in this moment (acknowledging that this answer may change over time as you change)? Note that there is a difference between "None of them are true" and "They are unimportant." Each path very much has something beautiful to contribute. What is important is that you show up, that you connect with the joy in your heart and trust it enough to enter into the unique role you came to play. Coming together in community gives us courage to play our respective roles by seeing the very human struggles we each have, no matter our background or spiritual path.

Each of the spiritual paths is important, like diverse birth stones that are meant to adorn a crown. They are beautiful by themselves, enough so that an individual can justifiably spend their whole life in devotion to just one. However, the truths in these spiritual paths were not entrusted to each culture as an endpoint for progression, but for safekeeping until the crown was ready to be assembled. We honor ourselves and our past generations by presenting the truths that were entrusted to us to be part of the crown. We honor ourselves and them by letting go of the past in remembrance of the future. Their sacrifices and journeys of faith were for this purpose, so that we, in our generation, could begin to assemble the fuller picture.

Individual growth is ongoing, but when we come into community of like minds and hearts, it is accelerated. The elephant moves when the legs decide to be part of the whole. Likewise, the car moves when the gas pedal is integrated into the vehicle. Our differences actually enhance that rate of growth by showing us that which we have not considered yet. It is a learning that almost takes place beneath the conscious mind, something that happens merely by occupying the same space, physically or spiritually, with others. This is how we evolve spiritually on a global level, going from a world of divided light into one great whole.

The raising and exaltation of the frequencies of light in all their forms will give rise to even greater potential for growth. All light belongs in one great whole. We have the chance to master our own gate or path into oneness and then to experience the light from each of the others. Let us love and respect each other. Let us learn from all around us. Our growth is accelerated when we learn together. Let us open our hearts to know God wherever He is found and to allow a joy beyond comprehension to flow through us into the physical world around us.

It didn't seem like we had been talking that long, but the plane was already coming in for a landing. We decided to wrap the conversation up, exchanging a few friendly goodbyes.

The man beside me on the plane said, "For what it's worth, what you shared with me really helped. And I think it could help a lot of other people too. They might understand more than you realize. I hope you will decide to publish it."

"It's funny you say that. I think that's exactly why we had this conversation – to help me see just that. I just needed to see how to write the book in a different way. In fact, I might even use this conversation to write it! I'll just add a few more parts of the story that we didn't get the chance to talk about and go from there. It may be I needed this conversation as much as you did."

He smiled at the thought and as I started to get off the plane, he added, "Then, I look forward to reading the rest of it!"

An Invitation

I'm putting forth this book with the intention of instigating global conversation on how we grow together. For that matter, this book is not done. Heaven is not a destination. It is a journey. Just because I've had these experiences, doesn't mean I've arrived anywhere. I'm just a fellow-traveler with a few more interesting stories to share, stories that leave me wondering at what life has yet to reveal.

Not only is my story still in progress, but it doesn't contain the most important part – the story of each of you. Life is like a jigsaw puzzle with billions of pieces. Too much emphasis on our individual awakening can sometimes blind us to the rest of the pieces still being assembled. There are those who bring the pieces of their experiences and there are those who assemble those pieces in a way that unravels the mystery of godliness in the flesh. The work of assembly is both faster and more enjoyable when we each contribute the part that we hold *simply by choosing to show up*.

This is not another item on a "to do" list. It is simply what happens automatically when two or more individuals holding adjacent parts of the puzzle come together in the same space and time. Without any effort on our part, the divine recognizes the symmetry in the puzzle pieces of our souls and merges them as one, releasing joyful understanding, expansion, and healing for all. It is the feeling of delightful surprise as a light spontaneously turns on in both hearts. It is also like the joyful surprise of a child when we discover that someone from another way of life is holding a piece of the puzzle that unlocks the aching part of our heart with tenderness and mercy.

This process is facilitated as we open our hearts to allow sincere joy and understanding in those that we meet. We can honor them by truly listening with our innermost being. In this way, the work of assembly of the divine puzzle that was never meant to be borne by us alone is carried out by a More Intelligent Love. To that purpose, I have gathered with others who have stories and interests like mine. While not all stories are as dramatic with visions of heaven, each story of awakening – even and especially those that are still in process – are just as raw in facing life's challenges and coming to an understanding that what we were taught is insufficient for what our hearts cry out for.

I recognize that for many people this book may have inspired deep reflection and desire for connection. It may also have raised more questions than it has answered, particularly with respect to where you go next and how you continue your journey. Start by doing the one thing you always wished those around you would do, listen to your own heart with love. Listen to what it is telling you. If you find that you still need tools or association with others to take the next step, consider connecting with us at Inner World Movement. A few of my associates, Dana Parker, Natalia Yates, and Hannah Foust, each of whom have gone through similar personal evolutions, are working with me to provide experiences, activities, and information to help you with next steps on your journey. It is a work in progress, so check back in with us frequently. In an excerpt of a conversation between the four of us, Dana answered how she would like to receive each of you in your journey:

Natalia: What would you say to people who have just walked through the gate?

Dana: It's one of those moments for me, I see myself welcoming people. It's just tears and hugs and love. It's hard to even put it into words because I know what it's like to walk through that gate. It's so heart-wrenching and difficult and yet so rewarding all at the same time, because there is so much expansion in it. That every part of me just wants to love on every person. Like, let's sit and have some tea together. Share with me your heart. I just want to know. I'll just listen and love you. I'd give them a warm blanket and just listen, and cry with them and laugh with them. And just empathize and be with them. It's like one of the most sacred moments you can participate with another human being. I'm not here to sway you or make you choose a way. I'm here just to love you and congratulate you. That's really what I want to do. Every part of me just wants to meet people and love them and sit with them. Just tell me everything. You're doing so good at this human thing. It's so messy and it's wonderful. Who has heard that in this life?

Brent: What you described is exactly what happens to people in near-death experiences. They come into the presence of God broken, shame-filled in many cases. There, they are listened to, understood, loved. What they don't know is that we can have that right now. We can have it in our own private spaces and in community. What you are describing is an aspect of heaven on earth, that feeling of being completely embraced and loved for all our humanness. We can give that to ourselves and each other right now. Heaven is here now.

The way I live my life may not fit everyone's preferences. I choose to have experiences and based off the results my heaven is expanded and refined. Whether those experiences work out or not, is not the point. The point is the growth and the learning that comes as a result of all experience. I choose to have those experiences that create understanding which liberates love without any force. I am inviting those who have the same passion for living, for understanding truth no matter the price to the existing structures in consciousness, to associate with us. If this path is not where your heart is leading you, then connect with others where your heart does lead. Connection is the important aspect here, first with your heart, and then with those around you. Find your tribe where your heart opens freely and fully, where your heart grows simply in the joy of being alive. Just connect, and through connection contribute to the global awakening.

Life is messy. Come be messy with us in a space where we learn to be truly without judgment, and where we can share tools to help each other in our respective journeys. Come be in process with us as the nature of life continues to unfold within and around us. Whether with us or somewhere else, find the people where your heart truly blossoms in this moment. Find joy and learning in connection. Open to the possibility that life can be more. Allow it to be more. Allow a love without comprehension to open in your space and the space around you.

For More Information. Learn more about Dr. Brent C. Satterfield at innerworldmovement.com. For review copies, speaking engagements, appearances, bookstore readings, and interviews, please email info@innerworldmovement.com. For book purchases, find *Bringing Heaven Home* and Brent's other book, *Faith to Produce Miracles*, on Amazon.

If you enjoyed the book, please consider leaving a review on Amazon or sharing your thoughts in a blog post so others can share in your joy!

Made in the USA
Middletown, DE
19 May 2021

40071007R00126